New
Bilingual Visual
Dictionary

English–Arabic

Milet

Milet Publishing
Smallfields Cottage, Cox Green
Rudgwick, Horsham, West Sussex
RH12 3DE England
info@milet.com
www.milet.com
www.milet.co.uk

First English–Arabic edition published by Milet Publishing in 2017

Copyright © Milet Publishing, 2017

ISBN 978 1 78508 881 0

Text by Sedat Turhan & Patricia Billings
Illustrated by Anna Martinez
Designed by Christangelos Seferiadis

Printed and bound in China by 1010 Printing International Ltd, May 2024.

▶ **Animals**	4–20
▷ **Human Body**	21–23
▷ **Home**	24–37
▶ **Clothing & Personal Objects**	38–47
▷ **Tools**	48–51
▶ **Technology**	52–53
▷ **Food**	54–71
▷ **Transportation**	72–81
▷ **Plants**	82–87
▶ **Environment**	88–97
▶ **Space**	98–99

▶ **Sports**	100–105
▶ **Arts**	106–107
▷ **Musical Instruments**	108–111
▶ **Time**	112–115
▷ **School**	116–121
▷ **Numbers**	122–127
▷ **Shapes**	128–129
▶ **Colors**	130–131
▷ **Punctuation Marks**	132
▶ **Symbols**	133
▷ **Index**	134

100–105	رياضة
106–107	فنون
108–111	آلات موسيقية
112–115	الوقت
116–121	مدرسة
122–127	الأرقام
128–129	أشكال
130–131	ألوان
132	علامات الترقيم
133	إشارات
134	فهرس

4–20	حيوانات
21–23	جسم الإنسان
24–37	المنزل
38–47	ملابس وأشياء شخصية
48–51	أدوات
52–53	تكنلوجيا
54–71	طعام
72–81	وسائل النقل
82–87	الطبيعة
88–97	الطقس
98–99	الأرض والفضاء

falcon
صقر

eagle
عقاب

flamingo
طائر النحام

swan
بجعة

heron
طائر البلشون

pelican
طائر الحوصل

gull
نورس

swallow
طائر السنونو

lovebird
طيور الحب

crow
غراب

pigeon
حمامة

robin
طائر أبو الحن

stork
اللقلق

ostrich
نعامة

peacock
طاووس

sparrow
عصفور الدوري

parrot
ببغاء

wing
جناح الطائر

beak
منقار

owl
بومة

claw
مخلب

tail
ذيل

woodpecker
نقار الخشب

nest
عش

birdcage
قفص

vulture
نسر

egg
بيضة

feather
ريشة

pet
حيوان أليف

dog
كلب

puppy
جرو

pet bed
سرير حيوان أليف

collar
طوق

cat
قطة

kitten
هرة صغيرة

crest
عرف الديك

chick
صوص

hen
دجاجة

rooster
ديك

horse
حصان

donkey
حمار

camel
جمل

duck
بطة

goose
إوزة

turkey
ديك حبش

barn إسطبل

bull ثور

cow بقرة

calf عجل

pig خنزير

goat ماعز

sheep خروف

lamb حمل

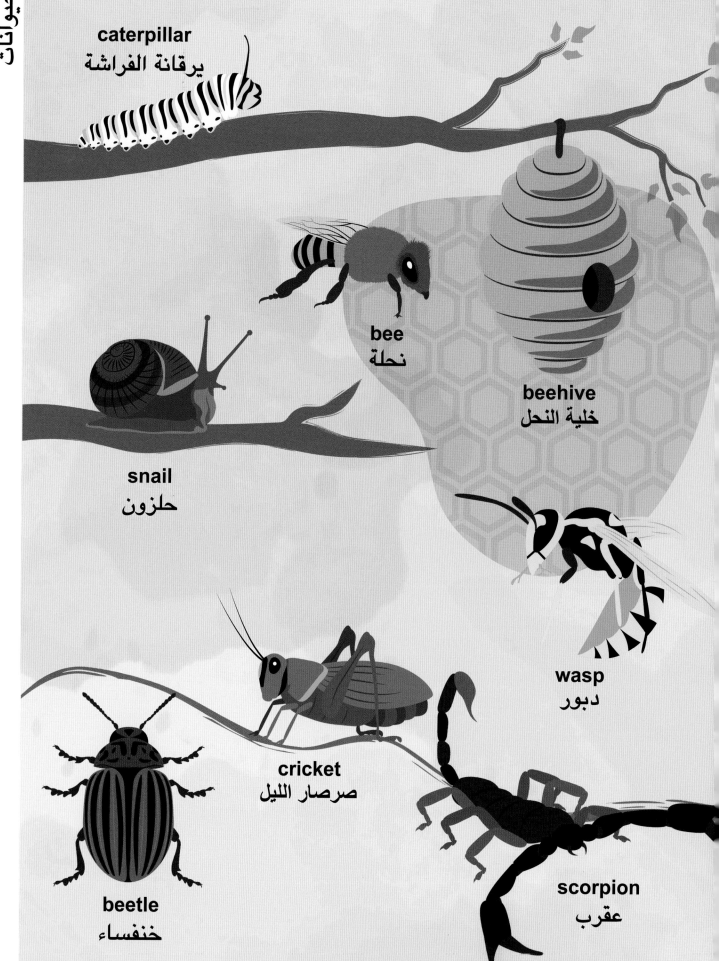

caterpillar
يرقانة الفراشة

bee
نحلة

beehive
خلية النحل

snail
حلزون

wasp
دبور

cricket
صرصار الليل

beetle
خنفساء

scorpion
عقرب

web
شبكة العنكبوت

fly
ذبابة

mosquito
بعوضة

spider
عنكبوت

dragonfly
يَعسوب

moth
عُثَّة

butterfly
فراشة

ladybird / ladybug
دعسوقة

grasshopper
جُندب

ant
نملة

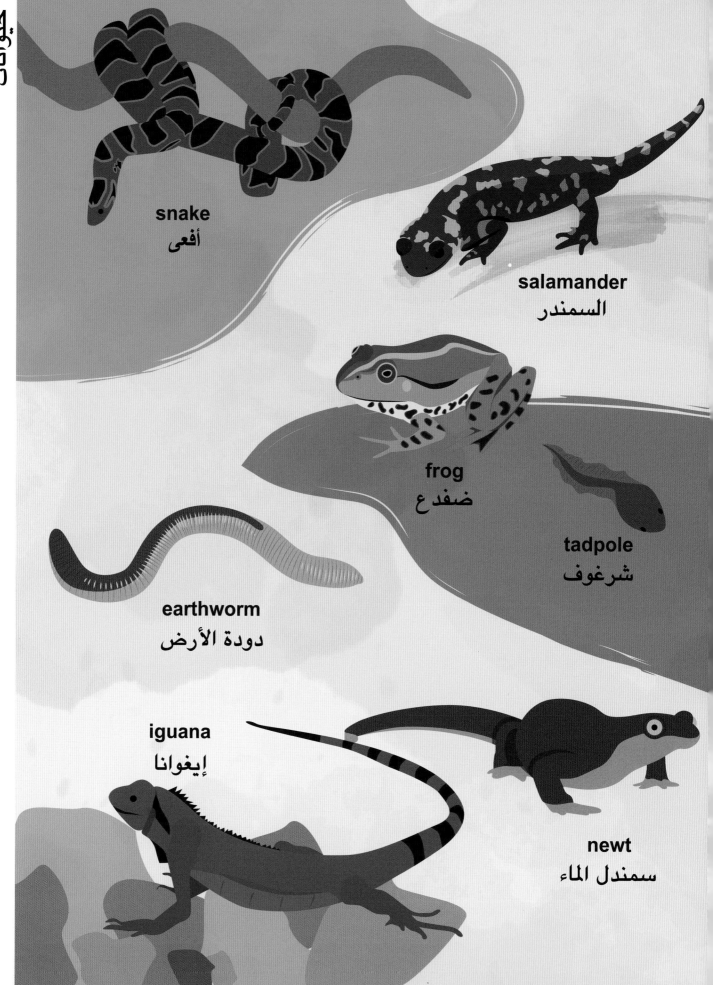

snake
أفعى

salamander
السمندر

frog
ضفدع

tadpole
شرغوف

earthworm
دودة الأرض

iguana
إيغوانا

newt
سمندل الماء

chameleon
حرباء

lizard
سحلية

crocodile
تمساح

toad
ضفدع

tortoise
سلحفاة

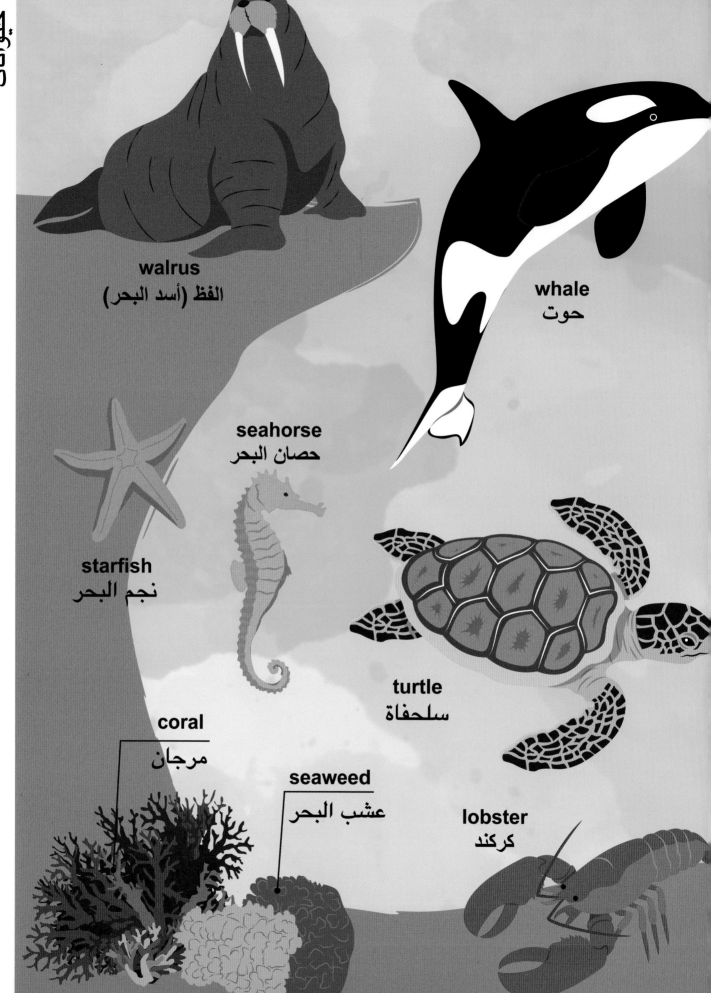

walrus
الفظ (أسد البحر)

whale
حوت

seahorse
حصان البحر

starfish
نجم البحر

turtle
سلحفاة

coral
مرجان

seaweed
عشب البحر

lobster
كركند

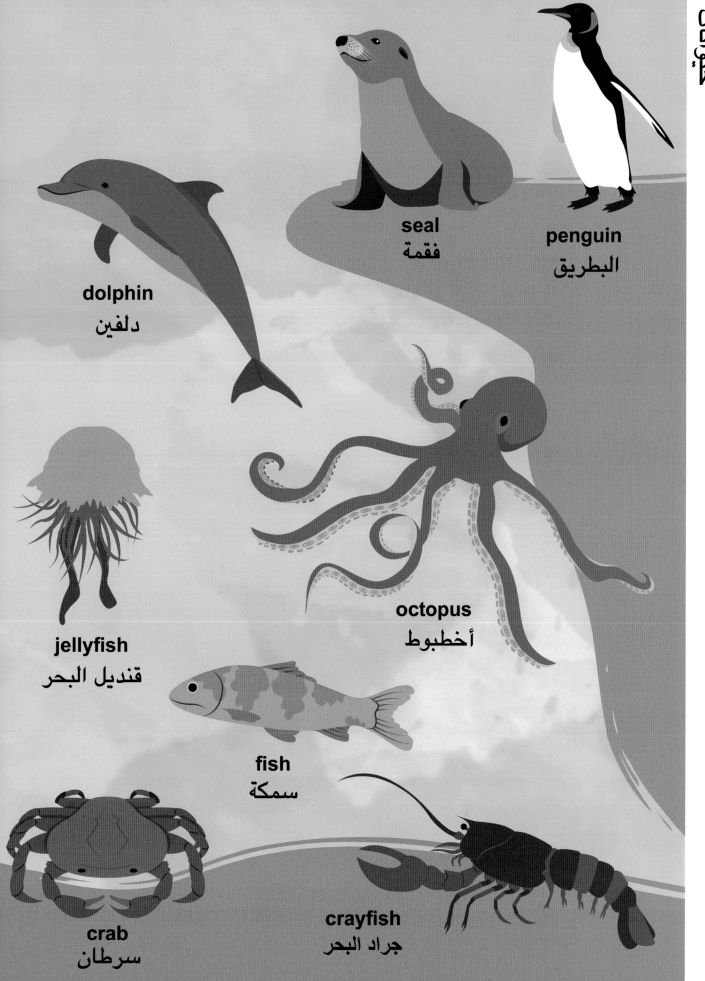

seal
فقمة

penguin
البطريق

dolphin
دلفين

jellyfish
قنديل البحر

octopus
أخطبوط

fish
سمكة

crab
سرطان

crayfish
جراد البحر

حيوانات

koala
الكوال (الدب الاسترالي)

bat
خفاش

kangaroo
كنغر

raccoon
حيوان الراكون

llama
حيوان اللاما

skunk
حيوان الظربان

16

bear
دب

polar bear
دب قطبي

elephant
فيل

tusk
ناب

trunk
خرطوم

panda
الباندا

fox
ثعلب

wolf
ذئب

chimpanzee
الشمبانزي

gorilla
غوريلا

zebra
حمار الوحش

rhinoceros
وحيد القرن

hippopotamus
فرس النهر

horn
قرن

fawn
الخِشف ولد الظبي

deer
الأيل

giraffe
زرافة

leopard
فهد

tiger
نمر

mane
بدة (عرف الأسد)

lion
أسد

cub
شبل

mole
خلد

hedgehog
قنفذ

mouse
فأر

tail
ذيل

rat
جرذ

squirrel
سنجاب

rabbit
أرنب

otter
قندس

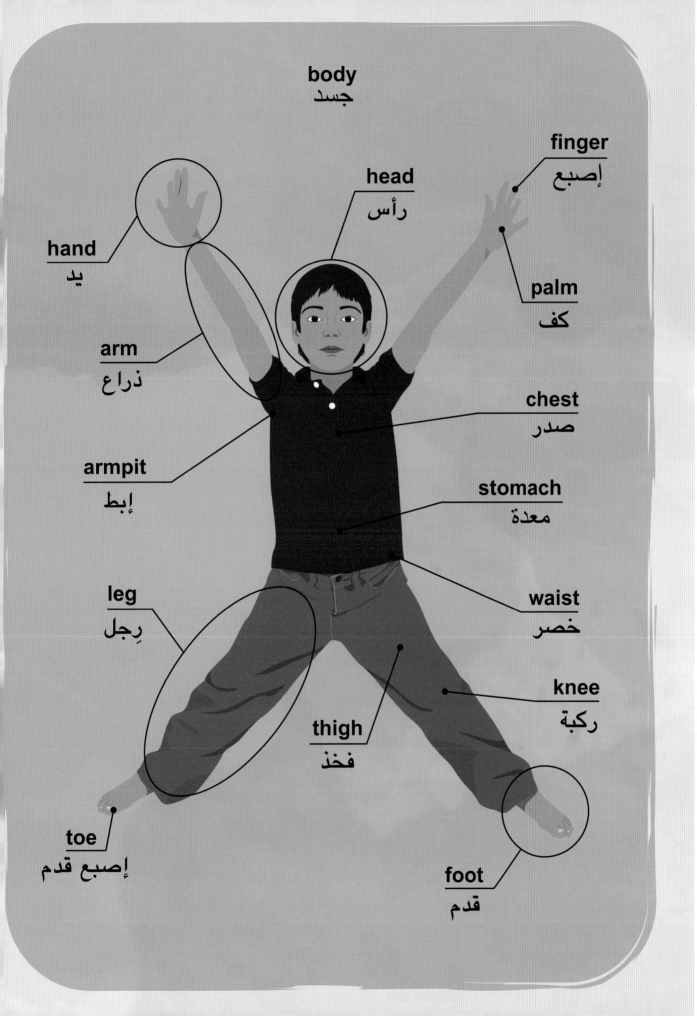

body
جسد

finger
إصبع

head
رأس

hand
يد

palm
كف

arm
ذراع

chest
صدر

armpit
إبط

stomach
معدة

leg
رِجل

waist
خصر

knee
ركبة

thigh
فخذ

toe
إصبع قدم

foot
قدم

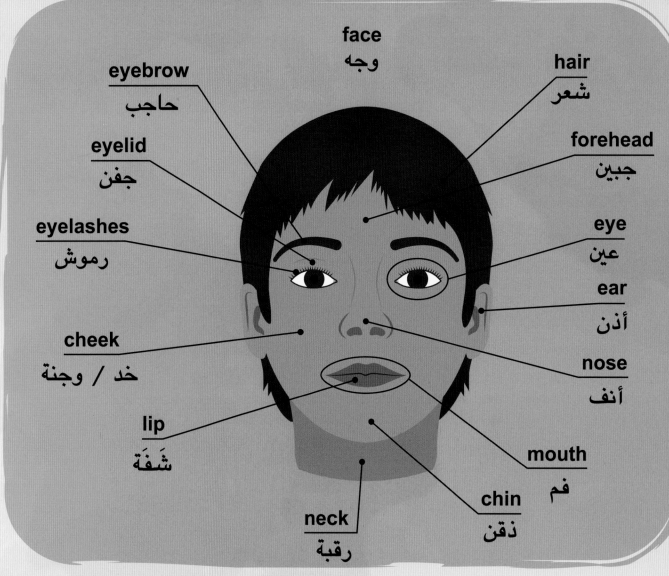

face
وجه

eyebrow
حاجب

hair
شعر

eyelid
جفن

forehead
جبين

eyelashes
رموش

eye
عين

ear
أذن

cheek
خد / وجنة

nose
أنف

lip
شَفَة

mouth
فم

chin
ذقن

neck
رقبة

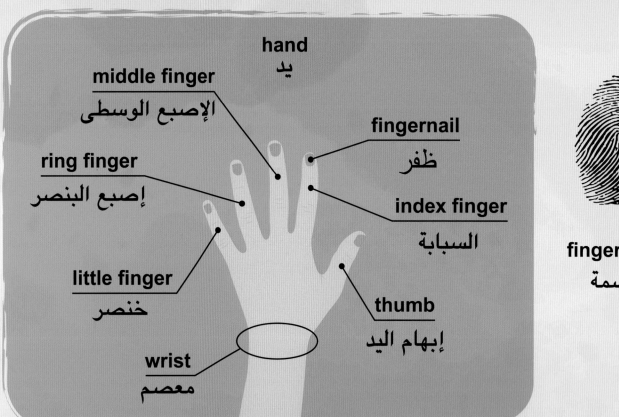

hand
يد

middle finger
الإصبع الوسطى

fingernail
ظُفر

ring finger
إصبع البنصر

index finger
السبابة

little finger
خنصر

thumb
إبهام اليد

wrist
معصم

fingerprint
بصمة

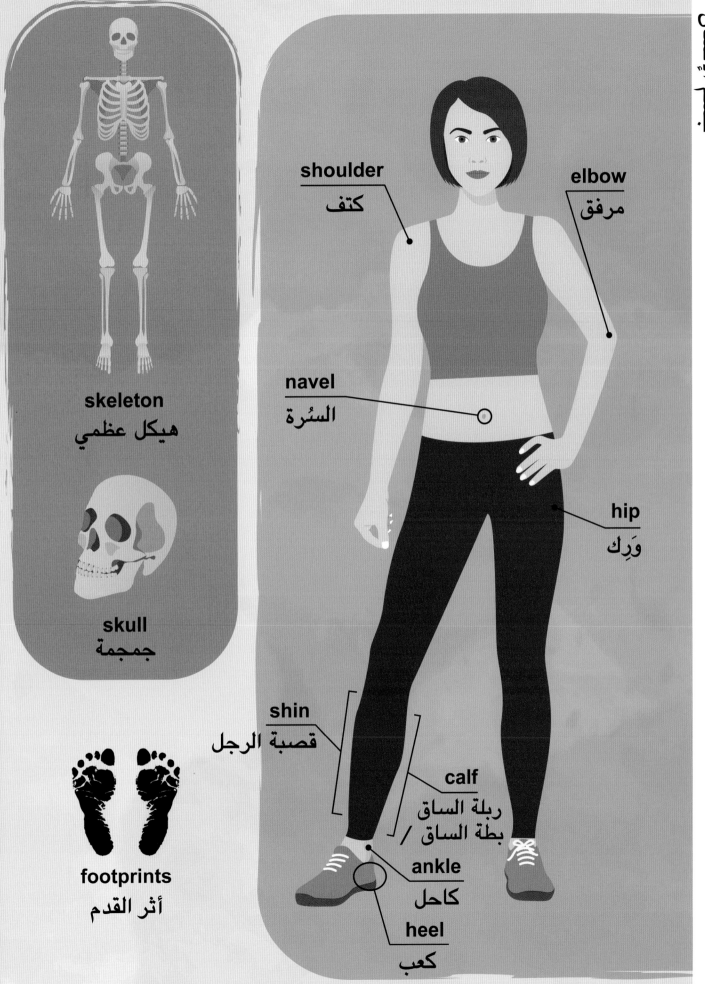

skeleton
هيكل عظمي

skull
جمجمة

footprints
أثر القدم

shoulder
كتف

elbow
مرفق

navel
السُرة

hip
وَرِك

shin
قصبة الرجل

calf
ربلة الساق
بطة الساق /

ankle
كاحل

heel
كعب

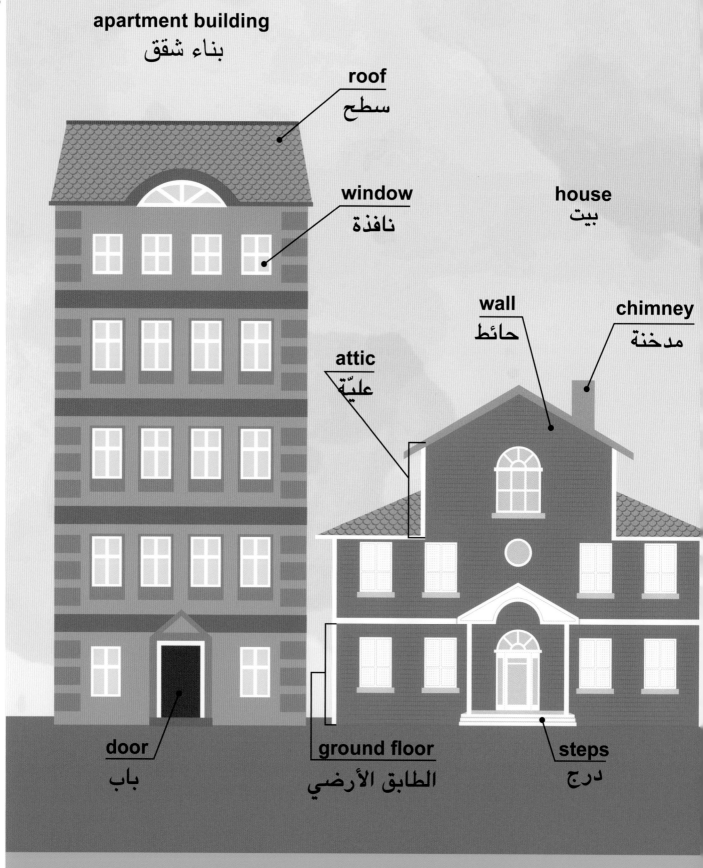

apartment building
بناء شقق

roof
سطح

window
نافذة

house
بيت

wall
حائط

chimney
مدخنة

attic
عليّة

door
باب

ground floor
الطابق الأرضي

steps
درج

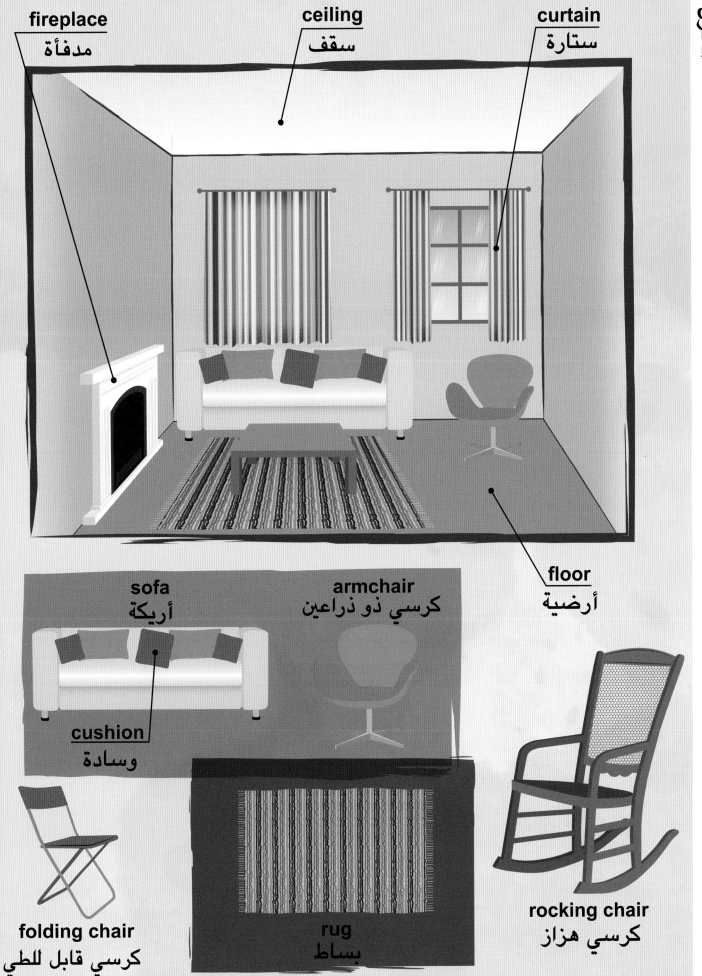

fireplace
مدفأة

ceiling
سقف

curtain
ستارة

floor
أرضية

sofa
أريكة

armchair
كرسي ذو ذراعين

cushion
وسادة

folding chair
كرسي قابل للطي

rug
بساط

rocking chair
كرسي هزاز

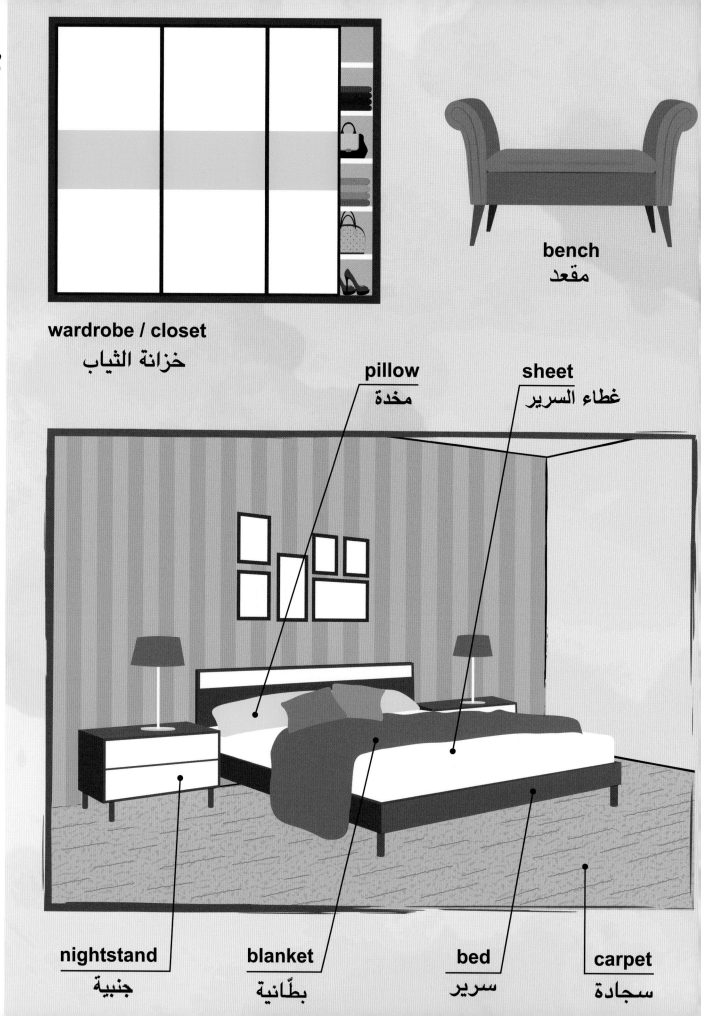

bench
مقعد

wardrobe / closet
خزانة الثياب

pillow
مخدة

sheet
غطاء السرير

nightstand
جنبية

blanket
بطّانية

bed
سرير

carpet
سجادة

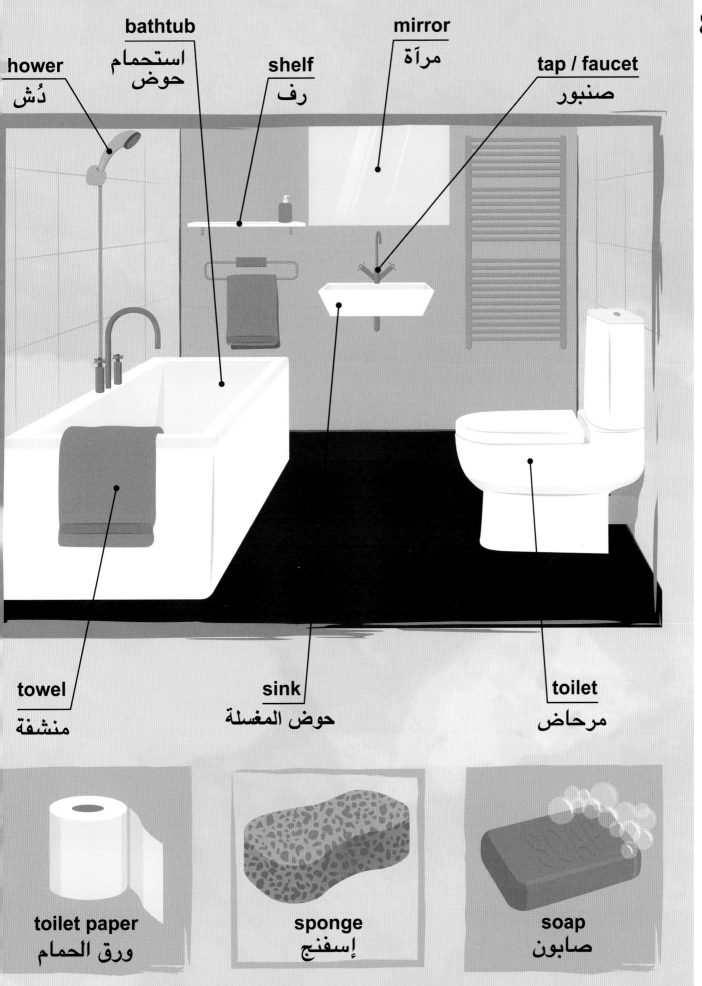

hower
دُش

bathtub
استحمام
حوض

shelf
رف

mirror
مرآة

tap / faucet
صنبور

towel
منشفة

sink
حوض المغسلة

toilet
مرحاض

toilet paper
ورق الحمام

sponge
إسفنج

soap
صابون

console
رفوف مثبتة

chair
كرسي

ceiling lamp
مصباح سقفي

dining table
مائدة طعام

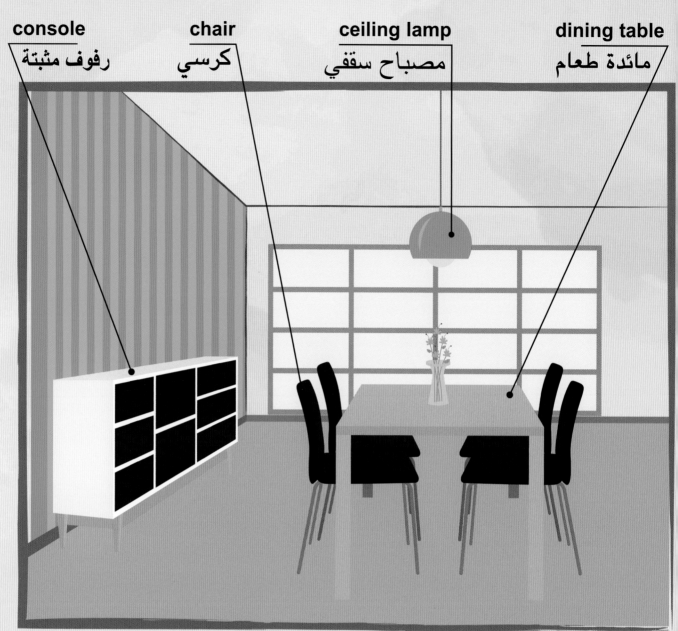

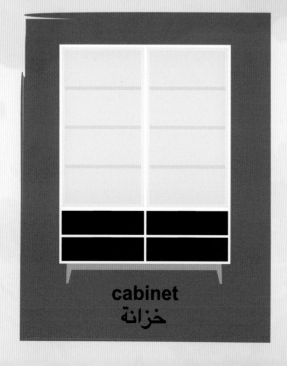

cabinet
خزانة

place setting
مساحة الطعام

stool
كرسي مرتفع

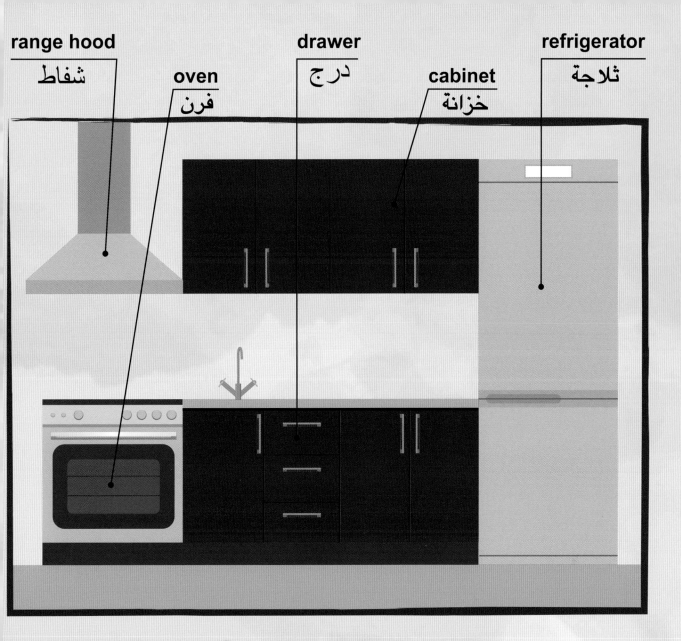

range hood
شفاط

oven
فرن

drawer
درج

cabinet
خزانة

refrigerator
ثلاجة

frying pan
مقلاة

pot
قدر

bowl
وعاء

slow cooker
طباخ متوازن

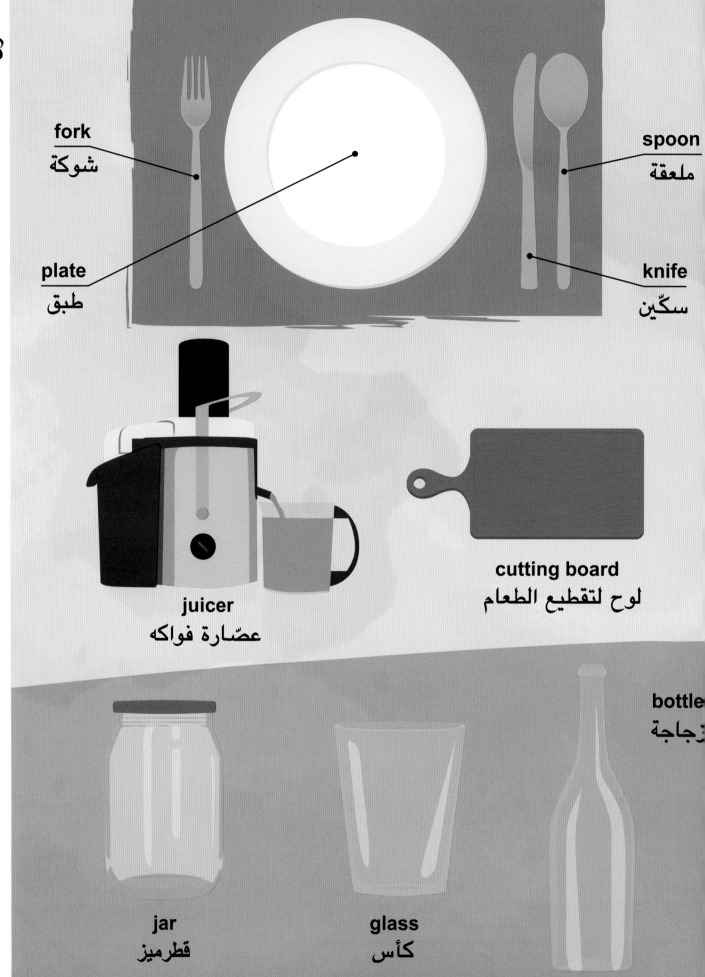

fork
شوكة

spoon
ملعقة

plate
طبق

knife
سكّين

juicer
عصّارة فواكه

cutting board
لوح لتقطيع الطعام

bottle
زجاجة

jar
قطرميز

glass
كأس

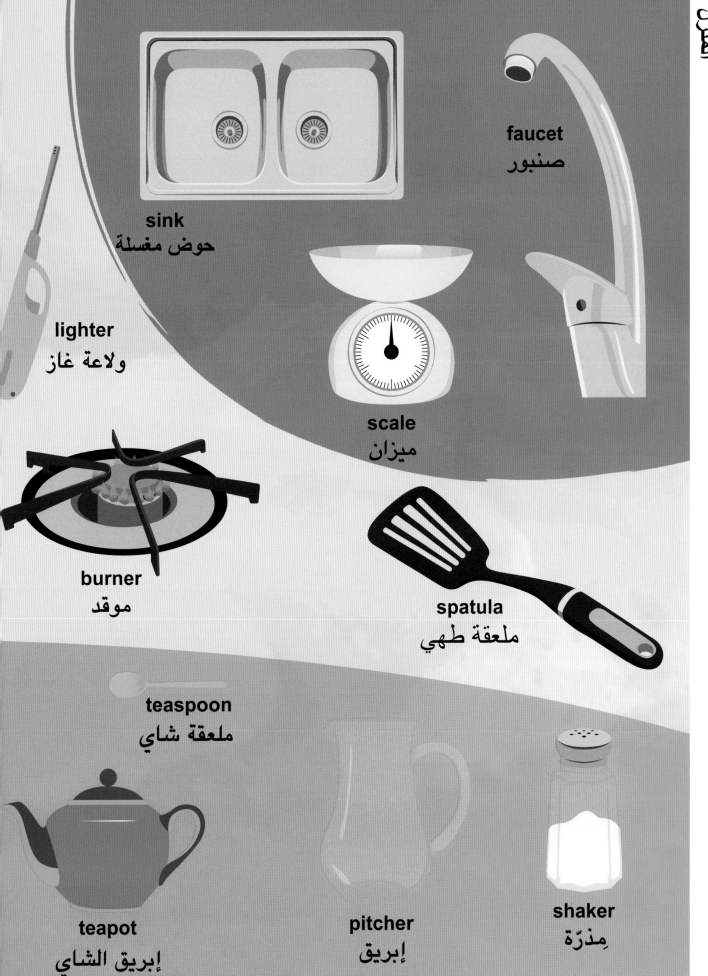

faucet
صنبور

sink
حوض مغسلة

lighter
ولاعة غاز

scale
ميزان

burner
موقد

spatula
ملعقة طهي

teaspoon
ملعقة شاي

teapot
إبريق الشاي

pitcher
إبريق

shaker
مِذرّة

mixer
مضرب مزج آلي

toaster oven
فرن تحميص

food processor
محضرة الطعام

blender
خلاط

toaster
آلة تحميص الخبز

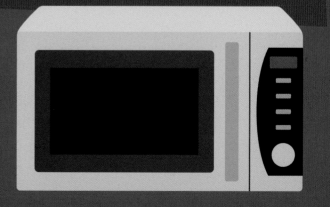

microwave oven
المايكرويف

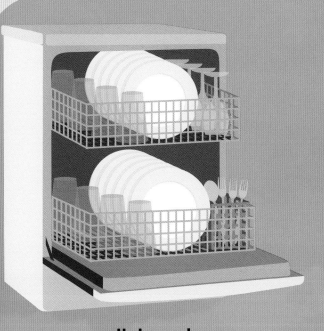

dishwasher
جلاية

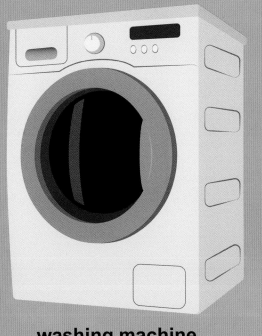

washing machine
غسالة

duster
منفضة غبار

iron
مكواة

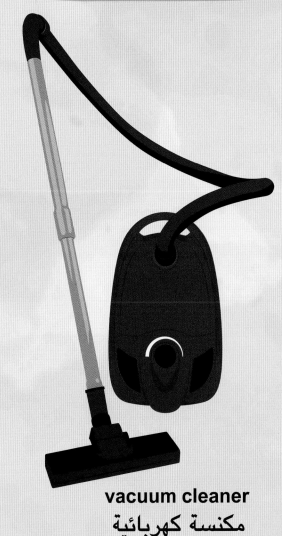

vacuum cleaner
مكنسة كهربائية

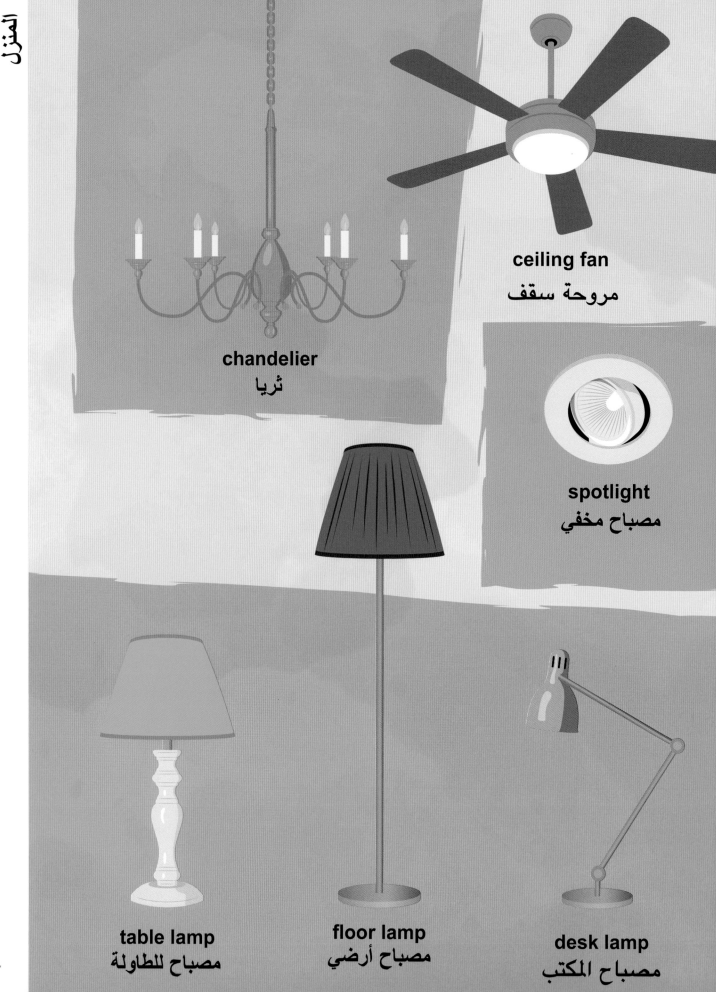

ceiling fan
مروحة سقف

chandelier
ثريا

spotlight
مصباح مخفي

table lamp
مصباح للطاولة

floor lamp
مصباح أرضي

desk lamp
مصباح المكتب

electrical outlet
مأخذ التيار الكهربائي

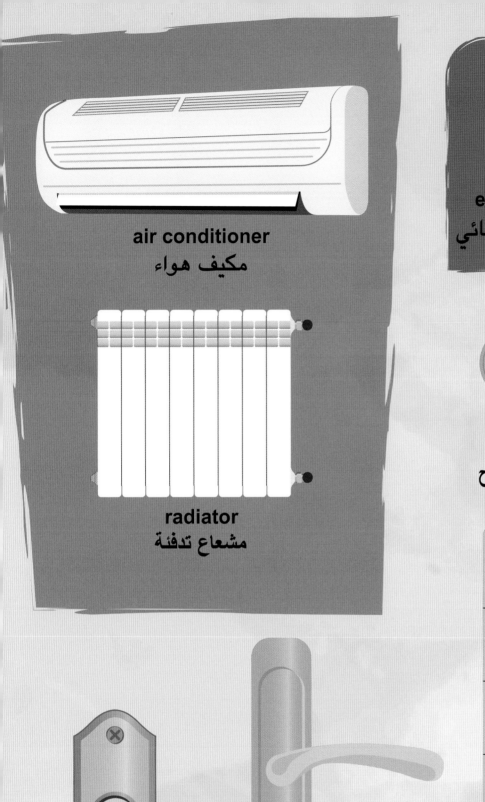

air conditioner
مكيف هواء

radiator
مشعاع تدفئة

key
مفتاح

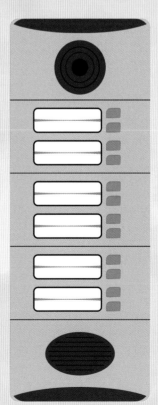

door handle
مقبض الباب

doorbell
جرس الباب

door buzzer
جرس خارجي

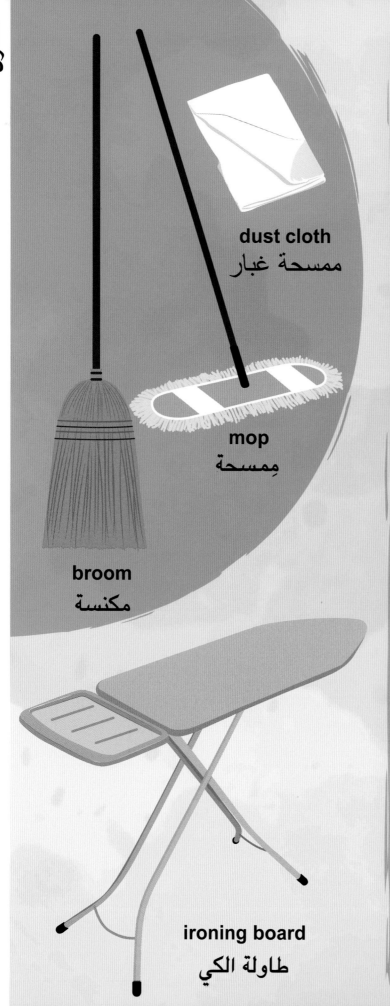

dust cloth
ممسحة غبار

mop
مِمسحة

broom
مكنسة

ironing board
طاولة الكي

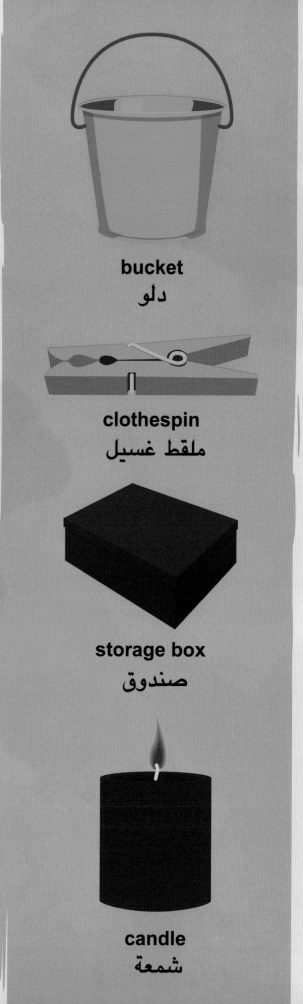

bucket
دلو

clothespin
ملقط غسيل

storage box
صندوق

candle
شمعة

flowerpot
إناء زهور

vase
مزهرية

jerrycan
وعاء لحمل الوقود

rubbish bag / garbage bag
كيس قمامة / مهملات

doormat
مِمسحة الأرجل

clock
ساعة حائط

basket
سلة

dress
فستان

blouse
بُلوزة

hat
قبعة

tie
ربطة عنق

skirt
تنورة

pumps
حذاء بسيط

bow tie
عقدة عنق أنشوطية

suit
بدلة

shoes
حذاء

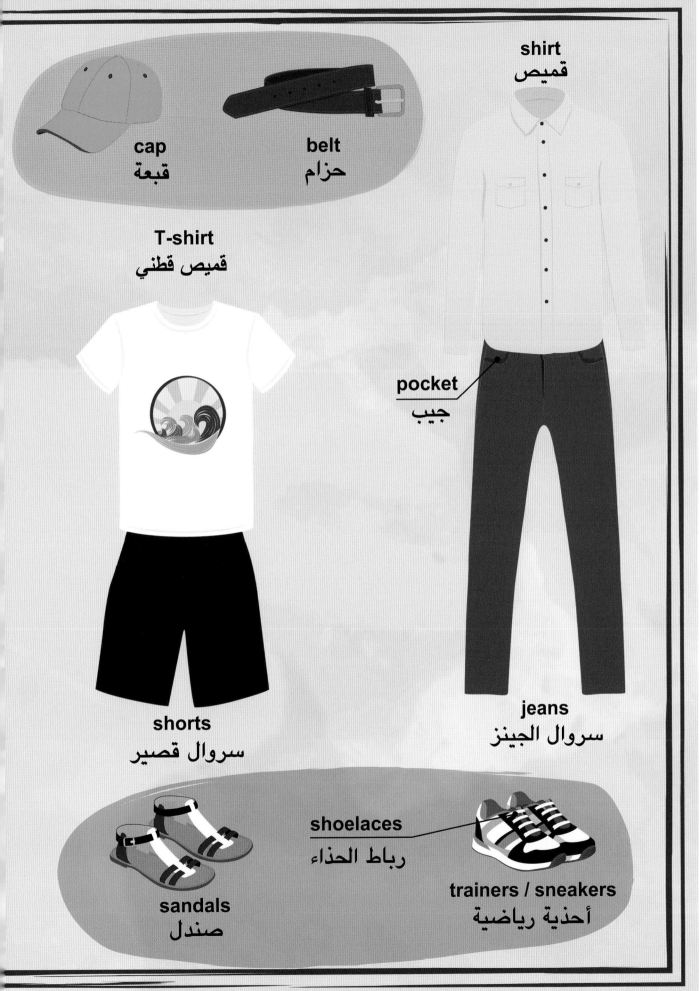

cap
قبعة

belt
حزام

shirt
قميص

T-shirt
قميص قطني

pocket
جيب

shorts
سروال قصير

jeans
سروال الجينز

shoelaces
رباط الحذاء

sandals
صندل

trainers / sneakers
أحذية رياضية

bathrobe
ثوب استحمام

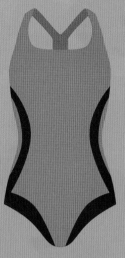

swimsuit
ثوب السباحة

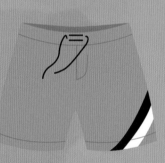

swim trunks
سروال السباحة

flip-flops
شبشب

slippers
خف

sweater
كنزة

cardigan
سترة صوفية

boots

حذاء طويل الرقبة / جزم

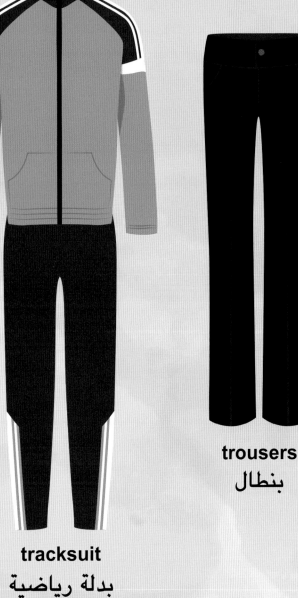

tracksuit

بدلة رياضية

trousers

بنطال

coat

معطف

gloves

قفاز

scarf

وشاح

socks

جوارب

clothes hanger
علاقة ملابس

ribbon
شريط

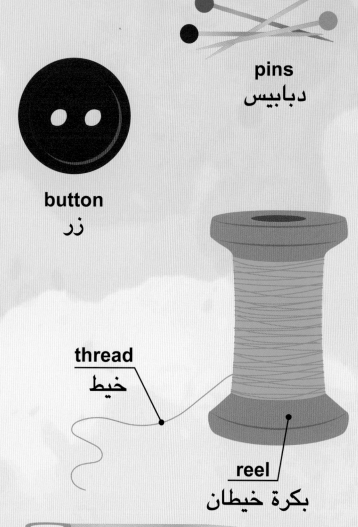

pins
دبابيس

button
زر

zipper
سحّاب

thread
خيط

reel
بكرة خيطان

sewing needle
إبرة خياطة

safety pin
دبوس أمان

eyeglasses
نظارات

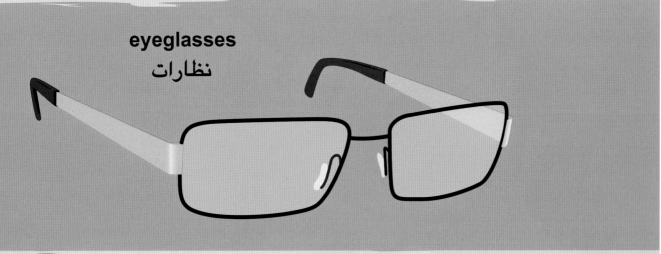

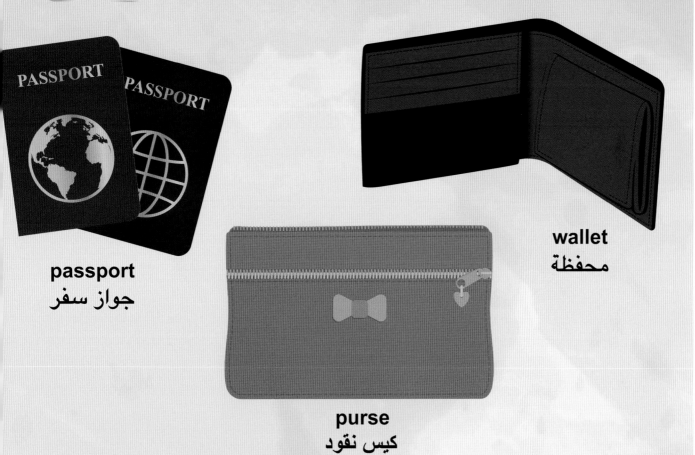

wallet
محفظة

passport
جواز سفر

purse
كيس نقود

sunglasses
نظارات شمسية

43

jewelry
مجوهرات

diamond
الماس

emerald
زمرد

ruby
ياقوت

earrings
أقراط

necklace
عِقد

bracelet
سوار

ring
خاتم

watch
ساعة يد

44

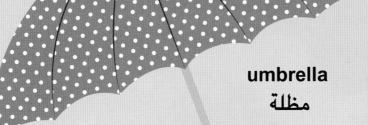

umbrella
مظلة

suitcase
حقيبة سفر

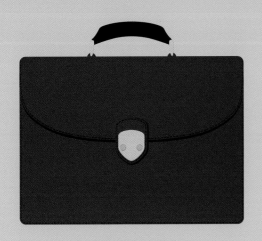

briefcase
حقيبة جلدية

handbag
حقيبة يد

backpack
حقيبة ظهر

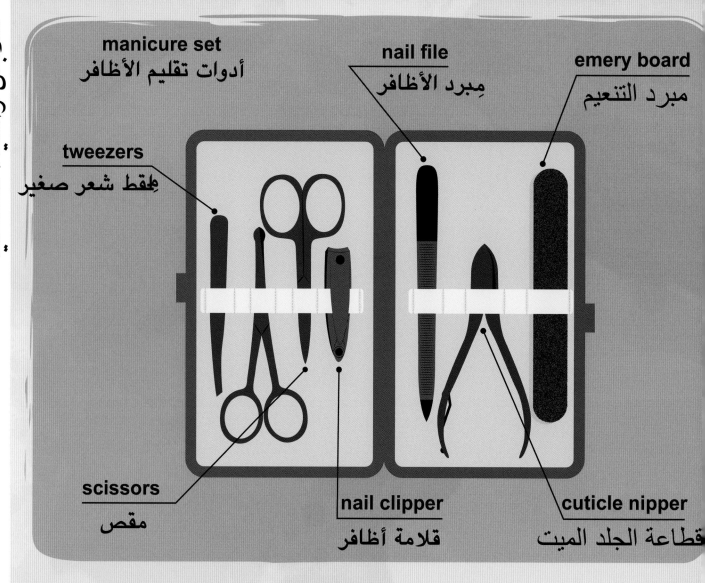

manicure set
أدوات تقليم الأظافر

nail file
مِبرد الأظافر

emery board
مبرد التنعيم

tweezers
مِلقط شعر صغير

scissors
مقص

nail clipper
قلامة أظافر

cuticle nipper
قطاعة الجلد الميت

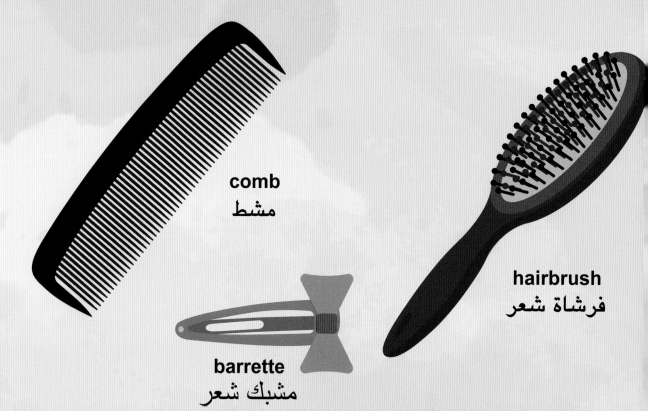

comb
مشط

hairbrush
فرشاة شعر

barrette
مشبك شعر

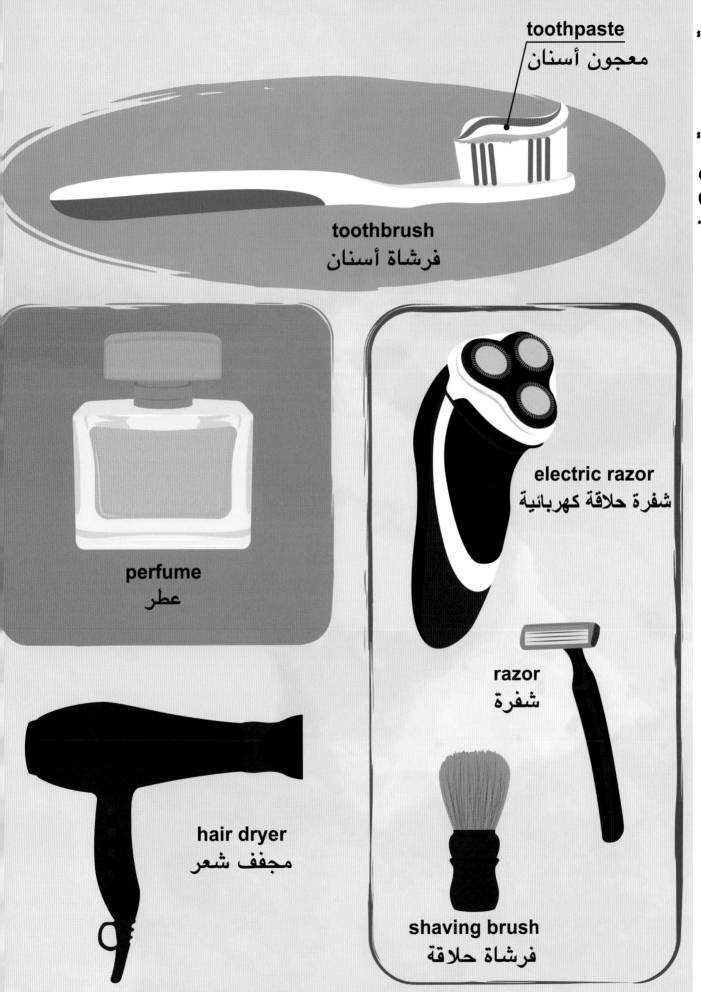

toothpaste
معجون أسنان

toothbrush
فرشاة أسنان

perfume
عطر

electric razor
شفرة حلاقة كهربائية

razor
شفرة

hair dryer
مجفف شعر

shaving brush
فرشاة حلاقة

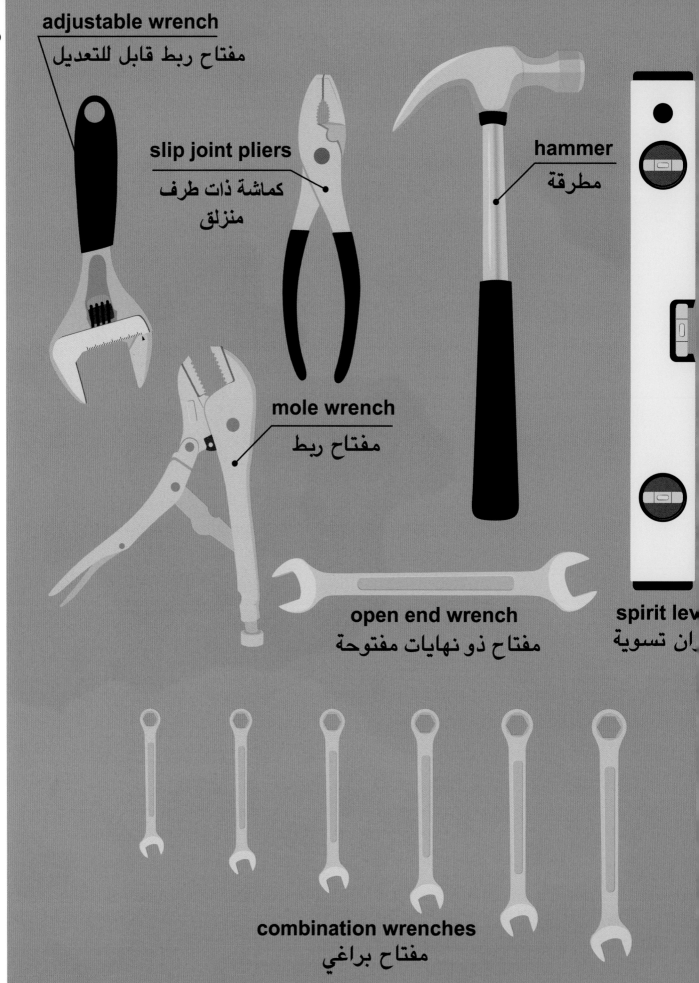

adjustable wrench
مفتاح ربط قابل للتعديل

slip joint pliers
كماشة ذات طرف منزلق

hammer
مطرقة

mole wrench
مفتاح ربط

open end wrench
مفتاح ذو نهايات مفتوحة

spirit lev
ان تسوية

combination wrenches
مفتاح براغي

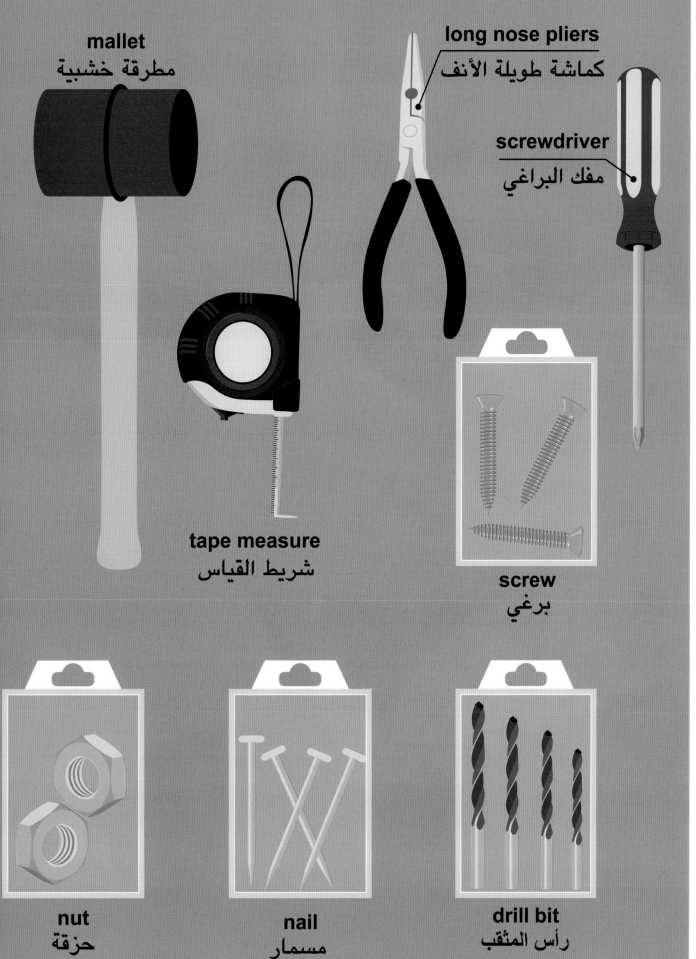

mallet
مطرقة خشبية

long nose pliers
كماشة طويلة الأنف

screwdriver
مفك البراغي

tape measure
شريط القياس

screw
برغي

nut
حزقة

nail
مسمار

drill bit
رأس المثقب

chain
سلسلة

plug
قابس كهرباء

padlock
قفل

battery
بطارية

toolbox
صندوق العدة

car battery
بطارية السيارة

electric drill
مثقب كهربائي

safety helmet
خوذة السلامة

torch / flashlight
مصباح يدوي

ladder
سلّم

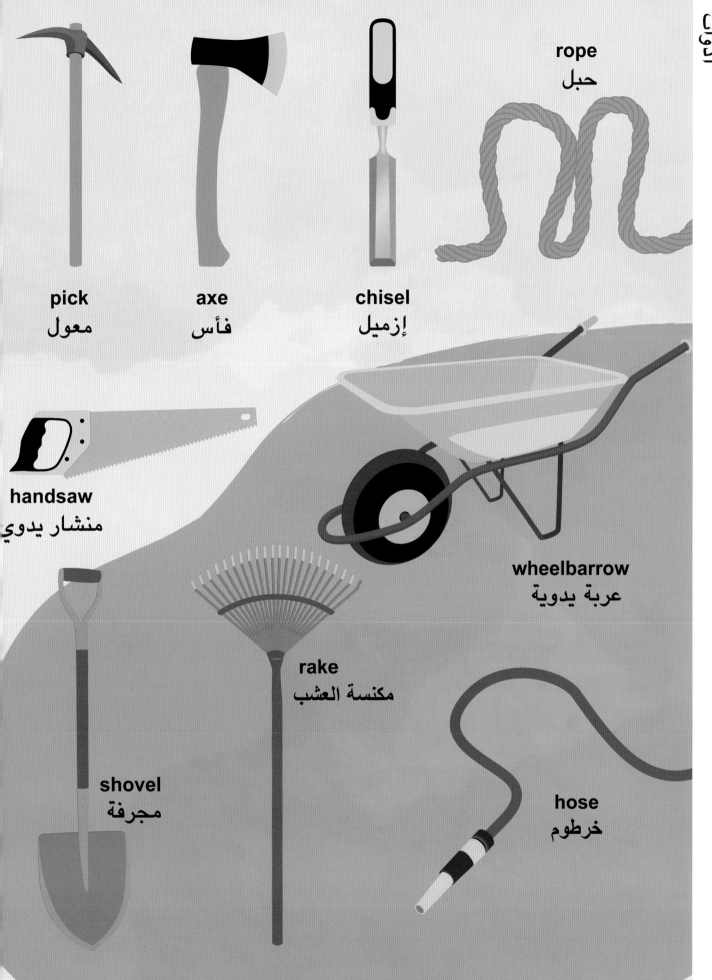

rope
حبل

pick
معول

axe
فأس

chisel
إزميل

handsaw
منشار يدوي

wheelbarrow
عربة يدوية

rake
مكنسة العشب

shovel
مجرفة

hose
خرطوم

monitor
شاشة كومبيوتر

speaker
مكبر الصوت

mouse
فأر

keyboard
لوحة المفاتيح

scanner
جهاز الماسح الضوئي

printer
طابعة

computer
كومبيوتر

video camera
كاميرا فيديو

tablet
جهاز لوحي

mobile phone /
cell phone
هاتف محمول /
هاتف خلوي

radio
راديو

microphone
ميكروفون

earphones
سماعات الأذن

cable
سلك

telephone
هاتف

53

supermarket
سوبر ماركت

restaurant
مطعم

grapes عنب

pineapple أناناس

lemon ليمون

orange برتقال

plum خوخ

watermelon بطيخ

apple تفاح

pear إجاص / كمّثرى

apricot
مشمش

peach
درّاق

banana
موز

avocado
أفوكادو

strawberry
توت

cherry
كرز

blackberry
ثمر العلّيق

blueberry
فراولة

raspberry
ثمر العنبيّة

kiwi
كيوي

mandarin
ثمر اليوسفي

grapefruit
الكريفّون

mango
المانجو

pomegranate
رمّان

quince
سفرجل

melon
شمّام

coconut
جوز الهند

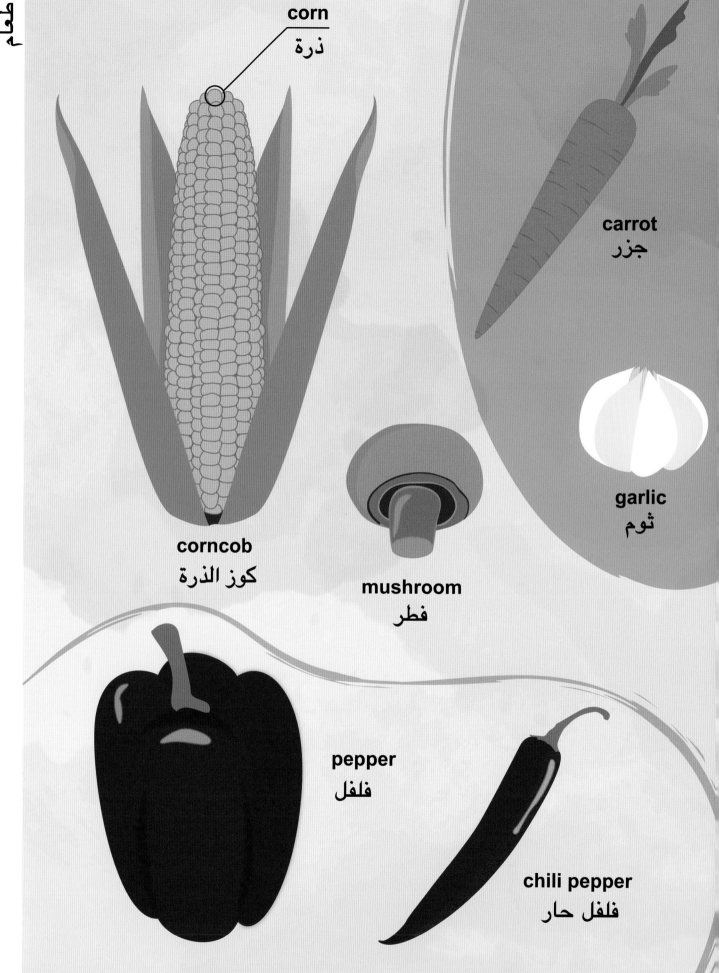

corn
ذرة

corncob
كوز الذرة

carrot
جزر

garlic
ثوم

mushroom
فطر

pepper
فلفل

chili pepper
فلفل حار

tomato
طماطم

cucumber
خيار

onion
بصل

pumpkin
قرع / يقطين

potato
بطاطا

green bean
فاصوليا خضراء

okra
بامية

peas
بازلاء

broccoli
البروكلي

cauliflower
قرنبيط

cabbage
ملفوف

lettuce
خس

artichoke
نبات الخرشوف / الأرضي شوكي

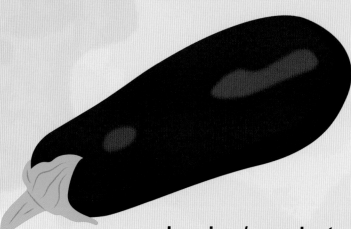

aubergine / eggplant
باذنجان

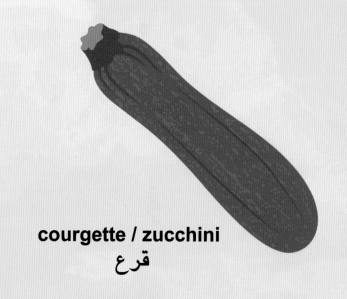

courgette / zucchini
قرع

green onion
بصل أخضر

leek
الكرّاث

celery
كرفس

spinach
سبانخ

turnip
لفت

asparagus
نبات الهليون

radish
فجل

dill
الشّبت

mint
نعناع

parsley
بقدونس

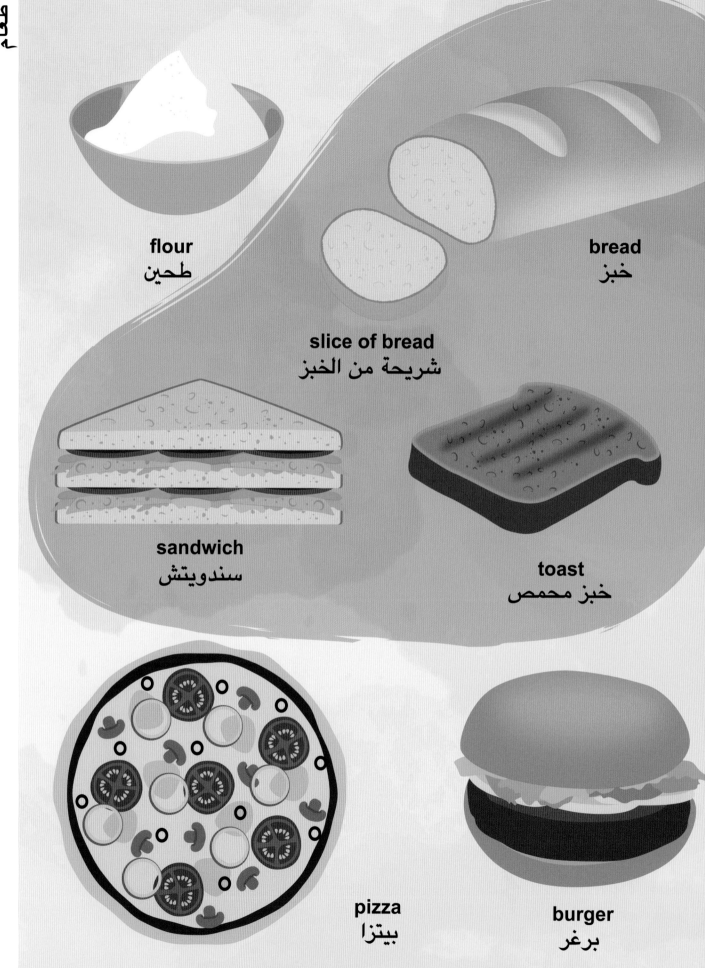

flour
طحين

bread
خبز

slice of bread
شريحة من الخبز

sandwich
سندويتش

toast
خبز محمص

pizza
بيتزا

burger
برغر

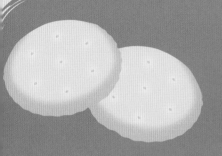

crackers
بسكويت رقيق

biscuit
كعكة صغيرة

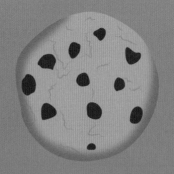

chocolate chip cookie
كعكة مع قطع الشوكولاتة

cake
كعكة

pie
فطيرة

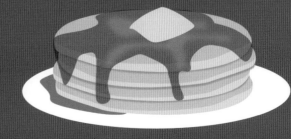

pancakes
فطائر

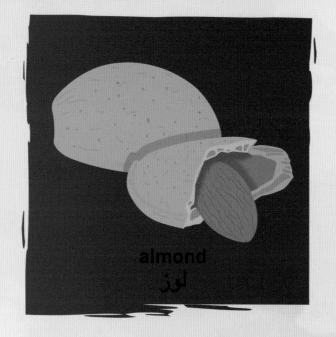

almond
لوز

hazelnut
بندق

chestnut
كستناء

pistachio
فستق حلبي

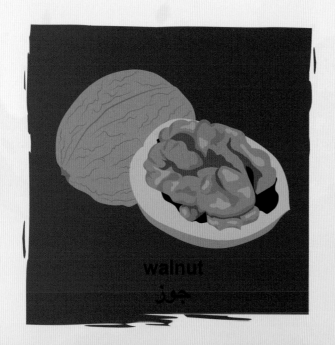

walnut
جوز

peanut
الفول السوداني

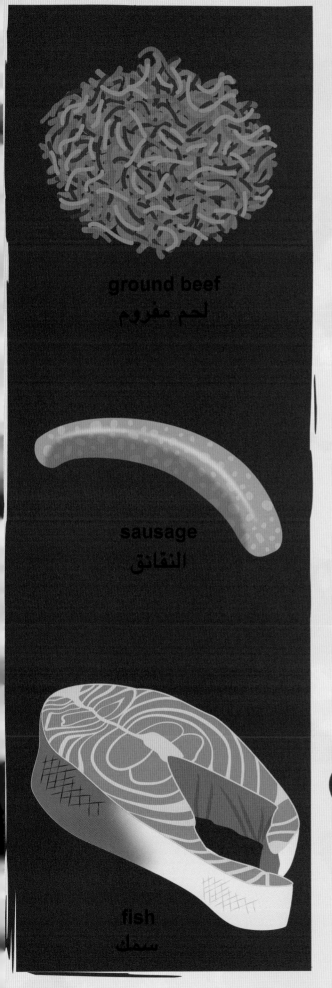

ground beef
لحم مفروم

sausage
النقانق

fish
سمك

chicken
دجاجة

steak
شريحة لحم

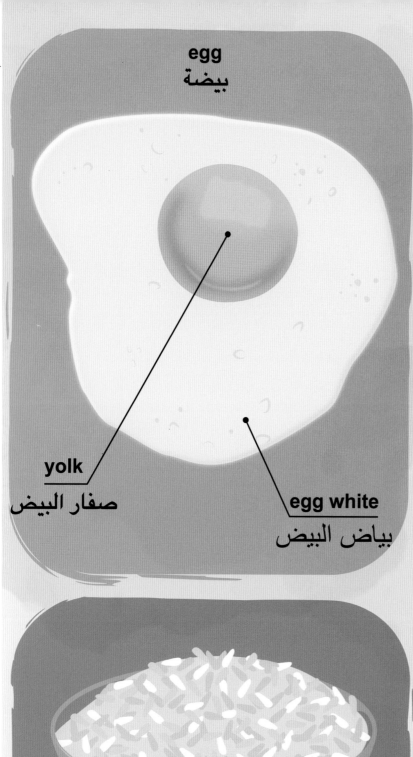

egg
بيضة

yolk
صفار البيض

egg white
بياض البيض

rice
أرز

pasta
معكرونة

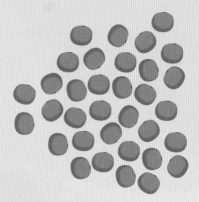

lentils
عدس

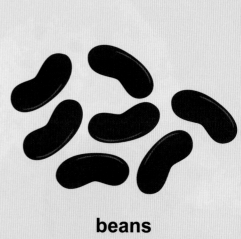

beans
فاصوليا

honey
عسل

canned food
طعام معلّب

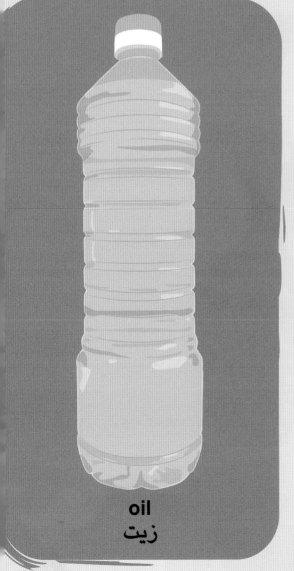

oil
زيت

olive
زيتون

olive oil
زيت زيتون

salad
سلطة

salt
ملح

pepper
فلفل أسود

snacks
وجبات خفيفة

soup
حساء

chips / fries
رقائق البطاطس المقلية

sugar
سكر

breakfast
إفطار

chocolate
شوكولاتة

candy
حلوى

ice cream
المثلّجات

dessert
حلويات

popcorn
الفشار

69

butter
زبدة

cheese
جبن

yogurt
لبن

soy milk
حليب الصويا

milk
حليب

water
ماء

fruit juice
عصير فواكه

lemonade
عصير الليمون

ice cube
مكعبات الثلج

orange juice
عصير البرتقال

coffee
قهوة

tea
شاي

car
سيارة

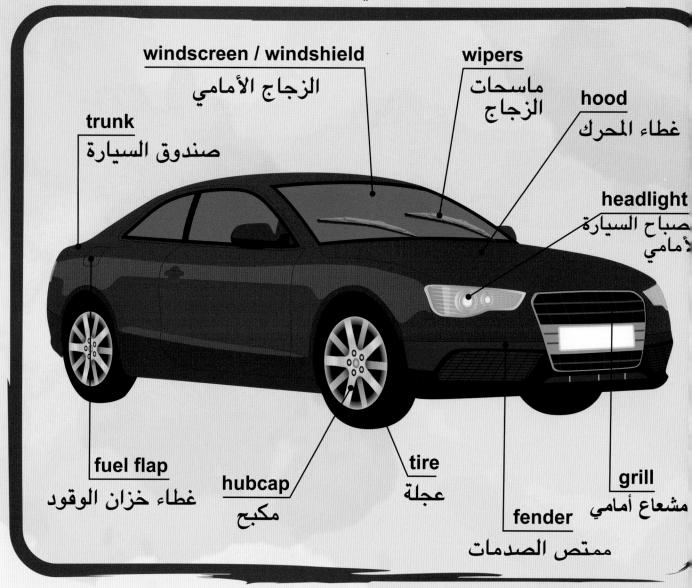

windscreen / windshield
الزجاج الأمامي

wipers
ماسحات الزجاج

hood
غطاء المحرك

trunk
صندوق السيارة

headlight
مصباح السيارة الأمامي

fuel flap
غطاء خزان الوقود

hubcap
مكبح

tire
عجلة

fender
ممتص الصدمات

grill
مشعاع أمامي

steering wheel
مقود

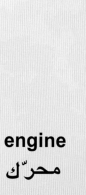

engine
محرّك

72

minivan
حافلة صغيرة

recreational vehicle
عربة تخييم

van
حافلة مغلقة

pickup truck
شاحنة بصندوق مفتوح

dump truck
شاحنة النفايات

tow truck
شاحنة لسحب السيارات

truck
شاحنة

freight truck
شاحنة مقطورة

bulldozer
جرافة

digger
حفار

forklift
رافعة شوكية

tractor
جرار

police car
سيارة شرطة

fire truck
سيارة إطفاء

race car
سيارة سباق

ambulance
سيارة إسعاف

74

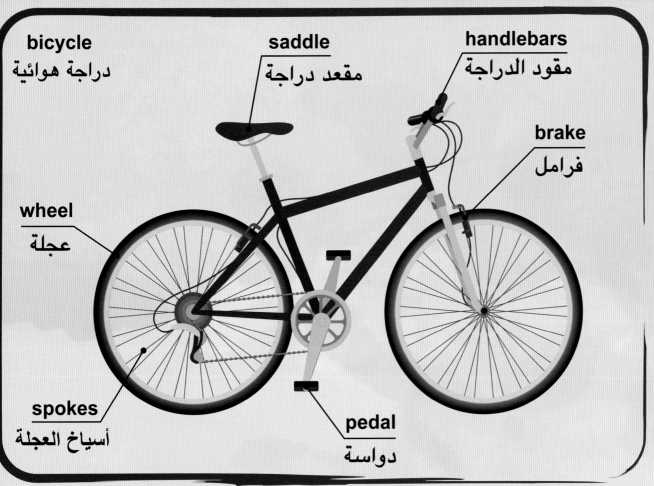

bicycle
دراجة هوائية

saddle
مقعد دراجة

handlebars
مقود الدراجة

brake
فرامل

wheel
عجلة

spokes
أسياخ العجلة

pedal
دواسة

scooter
دراجة بخارية صغيرة

motorcycle
دراجة نارية

stroller
عربة أطفال

sled
مزلجة

airplane
طائرة

wing
جناح الطائرة

helicopter
طائرة مروحية

bus
حافلة

76

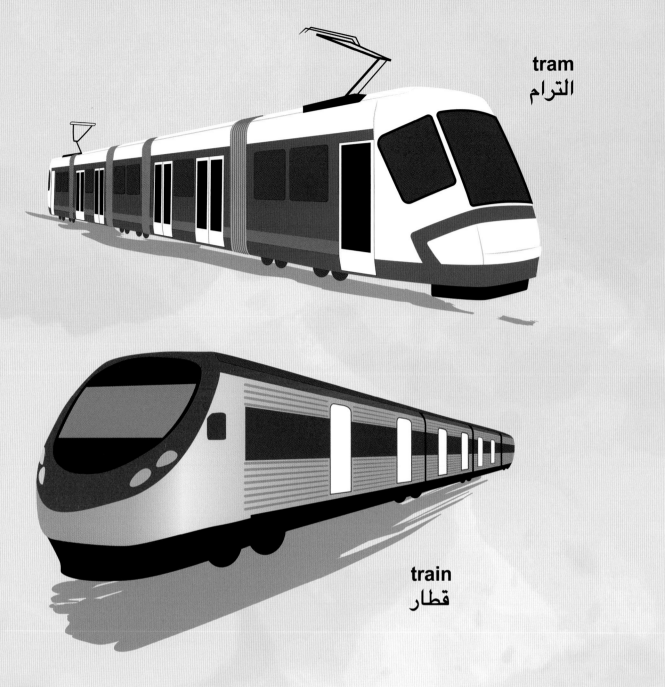

tram
الترام

train
قطار

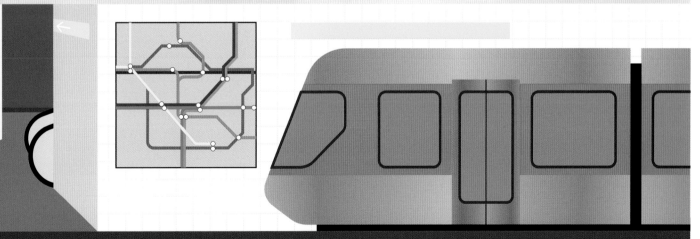

underground / subway
قطار الأنفاق

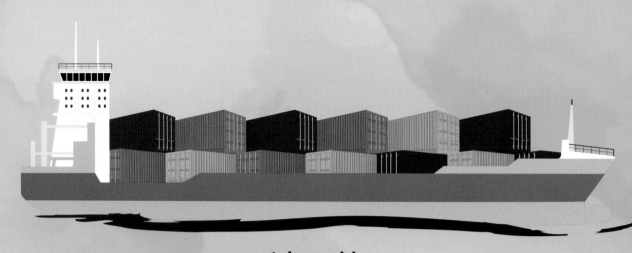

container ship

سفينة شحن

cruise ship

سفينة سياحية

yacht

يخت

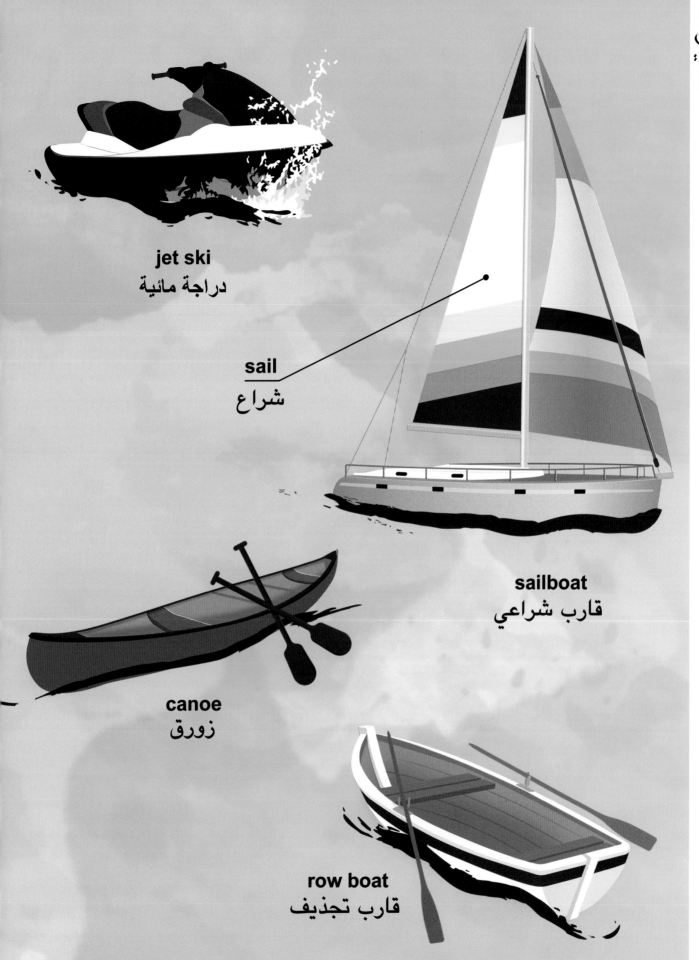

jet ski
دراجة مائية

sail
شراع

sailboat
قارب شراعي

canoe
زورق

row boat
قارب تجذيف

airport
مطار

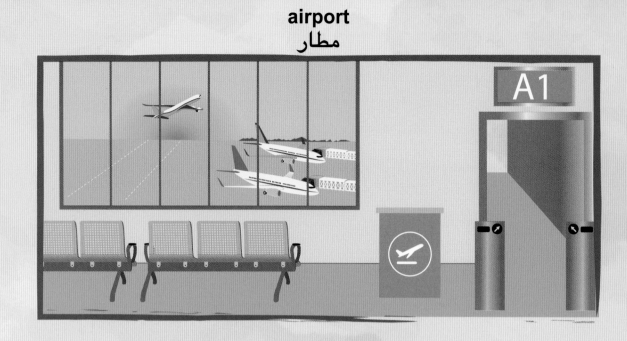

street
شارع

bus stop / **sidewalk** **crosswalk** **traffic light**

موقف للحافلات رصيف ممر مشاة إشارة مرور

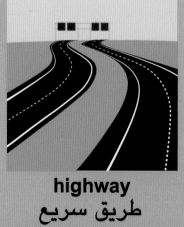

road **highway** **traffic**

طريق طريق سريع المرور

garage
مرآب

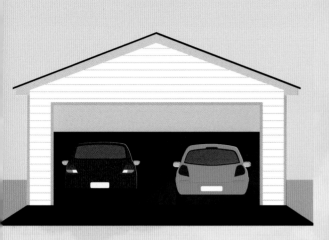

petrol station / gas station
محطة وقود

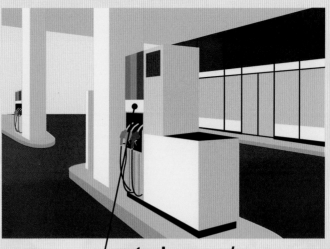

petrol pump / gas pump
مضخة وقود

train station
محطة قطار

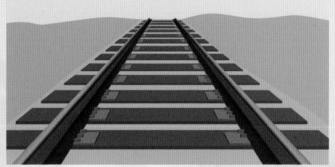

railroad track
سكة قطار

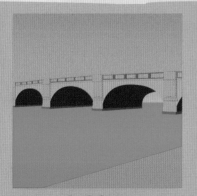

bridge
جسر

pier
رصيف ممتد في البحر

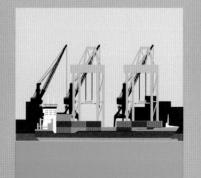

port
ميناء

fuchsia
شجيرة الفوشية

camellia
زهرة الكاميليا

daisy
زهرة الأقحوان

cotton
قطن

bud
برعم

begonia
البغونية

carnation
زهر القرنفل

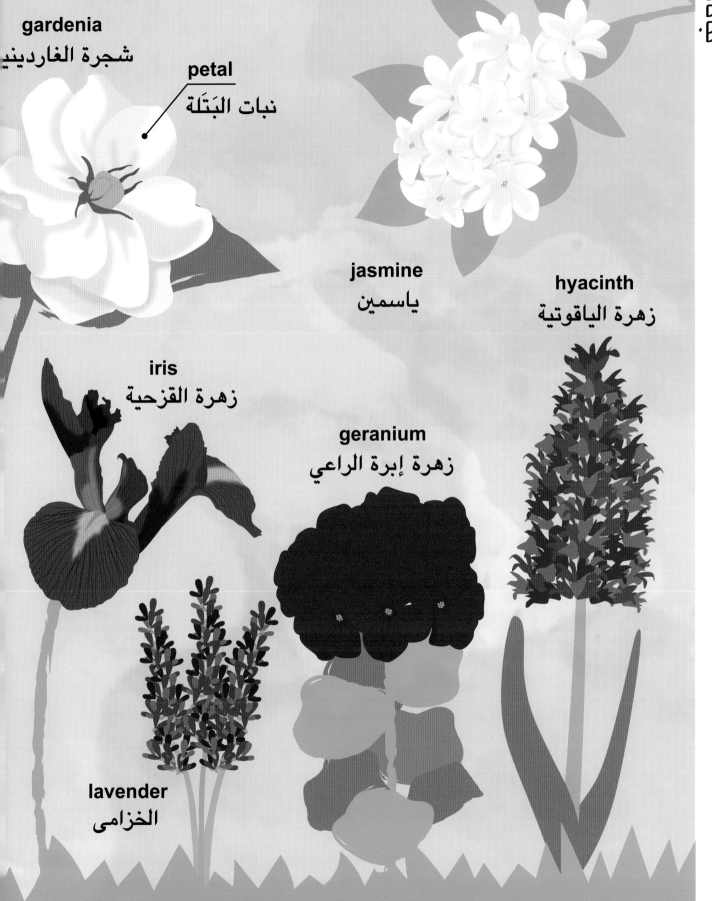

gardenia
شجرة الغارديني

petal
نبات البَتَلة

jasmine
ياسمين

hyacinth
زهرة الياقوتية

iris زهرة القزحية

geranium
زهرة إبرة الراعي

lavender
الخزامى

magnolia
الماغنوليا

snapdragon
نبتة أنف العجل

nettle
نبات القُرّاص

daffodil
زهر النرجس

poppy
زهرة
الخشخاش

lilac
زهر الليلك

moss
طحالب

grass
عشب

orchid
الأوركيد

rose
وردة

sunflower
زهرة عباد الشمس

tulip
زهرة التوليب

snowdrop
زهرة اللبن الثلجية

water lily
زنبق الماء

pine cone
كوز الصنوبر

oats
الشوفان

wheat
قمح

rye
الجاودار

palm tree
شجرة نخيل

cactus
صبّار

grape tree
كرمة

garden
حديقة

leaf
ورقة نبات

tree
شجرة

bush
شجيرة

branch
فرع

trunk
جذع

root
جذر

barn
إسطبل

countryside
الريف

farm
مزرعة

hay
قش

wood
خشب

log
رند الخشب

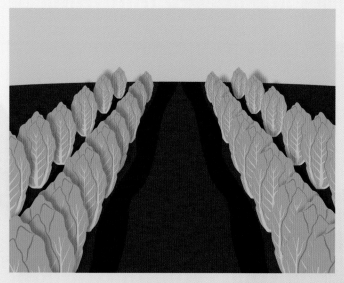

harvest
حصاد

field
حقل

island
جزيرة

sand
رمال

beach
شاطئ

lake
بركة

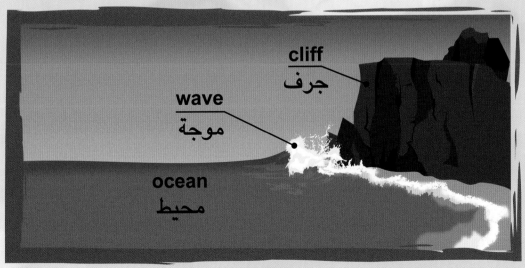

cliff
جرف

wave
موجة

ocean
محيط

coast
ساحل

wetland
مستنقع

dam
سد

waterfall
شلال

forest غابة

path
مسار

desert
صحراء

cave
كهف

jungle
أدغال

soil
تربة

fossil
مستحاثة

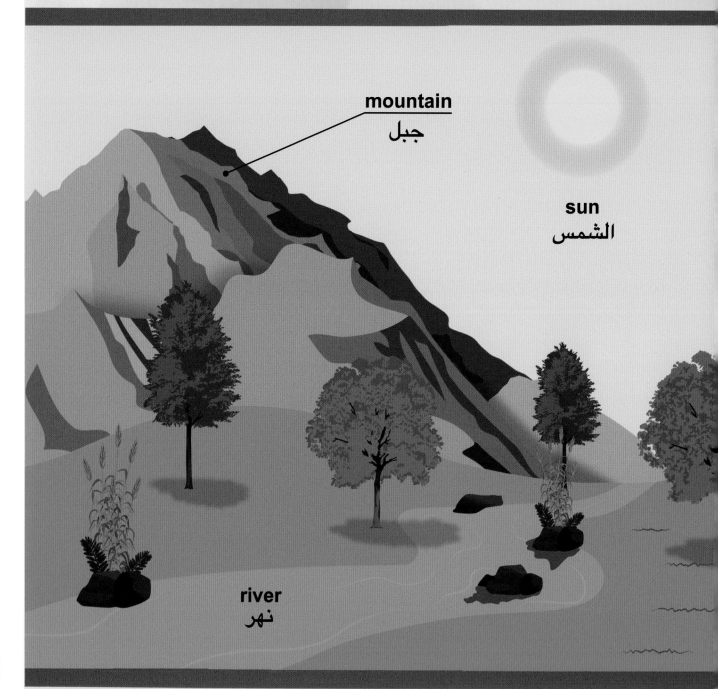

mountain
جبل

sun
الشمس

river
نهر

pebbles
حصاة

stone
حجر

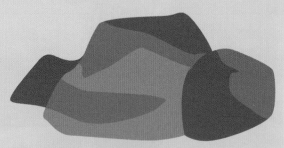

rock
صخرة

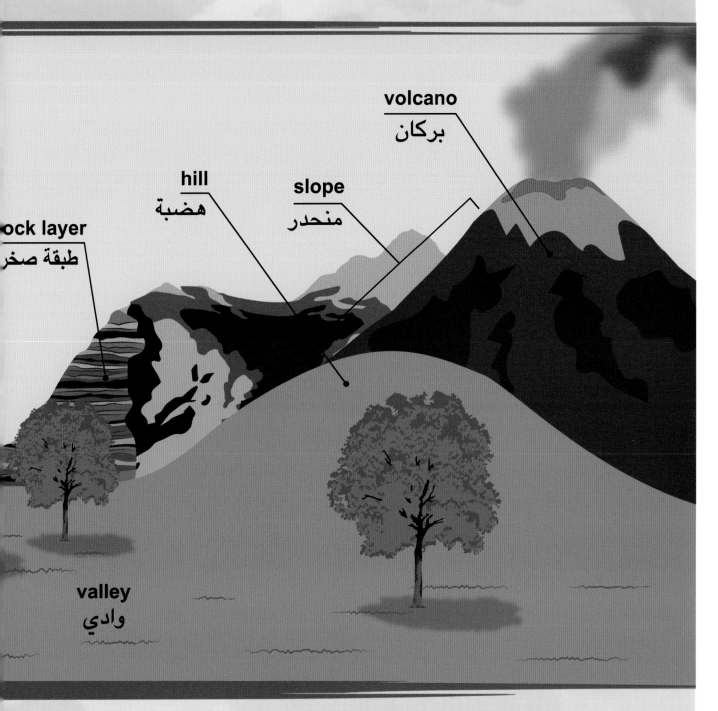

volcano
بركان

hill
هضبة

slope
منحدر

ock layer
طبقة صخر

valley
وادي

تَشارِيس

disaster
كارثة

hurricane
عاصفة

flood
طوفان

earthquake
زلزال

tornado
إعصار

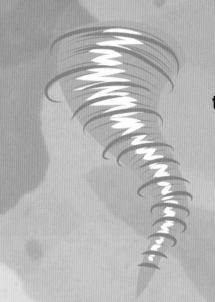

fire
نار

flame
لهب

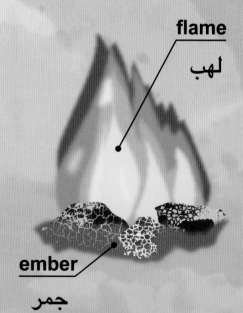

ember
جمر

94

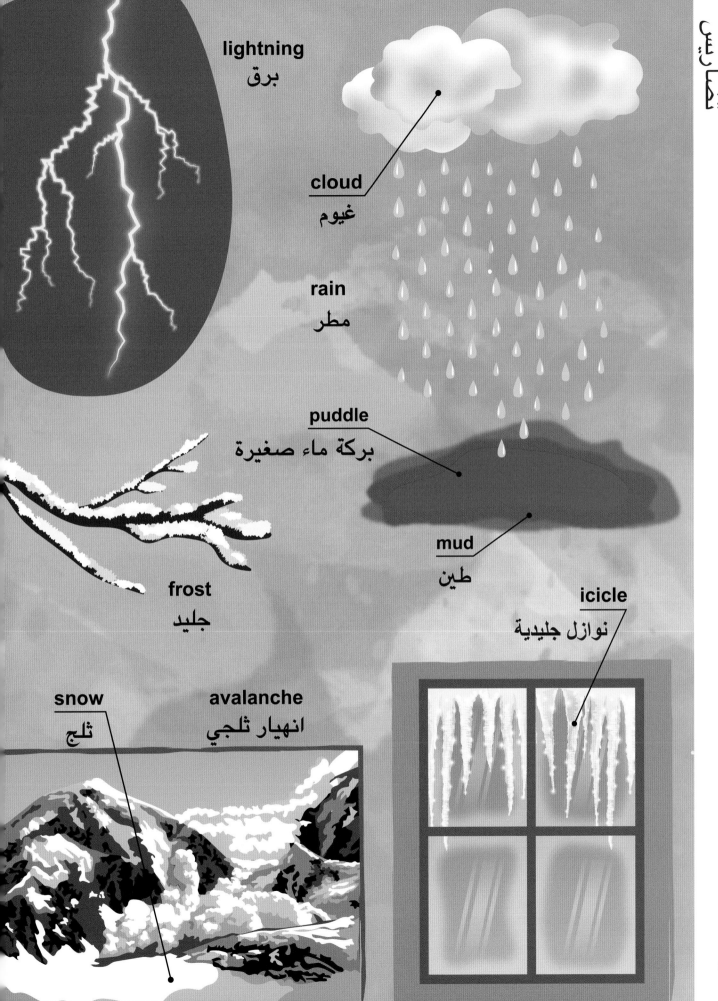

lightning
برق

cloud
غيوم

rain
مطر

puddle
بركة ماء صغيرة

frost
جليد

mud
طين

icicle
نوازل جليدية

snow
ثلج

avalanche
انهيار ثلجي

continents
قارات

North America
أميريكا الشمالية

Europe
أوروبا

South America
أميريكا الجنوبية

Antarctica
القطب الجنوبي

Asia
آسيا

Africa
أفريقيا

Australia
أستراليا

solar system
نظام شمسي

Moon
القمر

Venus
كوكب الزهرة

Earth
كوكب الأرض

Mercury
كوكب عطارد

Neptune
كوكب نيبتون

Mars
المريخ

Sun
الشمس

Uranus
أورانوس

Saturn
كوكب زحل

Jupiter
كوكب المشتري

galaxy
المجرة

space shuttle
مكوك فضائي

space station
محطة فضائية

satellite dish
لاقط فضائي

astronaut
رائد فضاء

American football
كرة القدم الأميركية

basketball
كرة السلة

weightlifting
رفع أثقال

archery
الرماية

wrestling
مصارعة

judo
الجودو

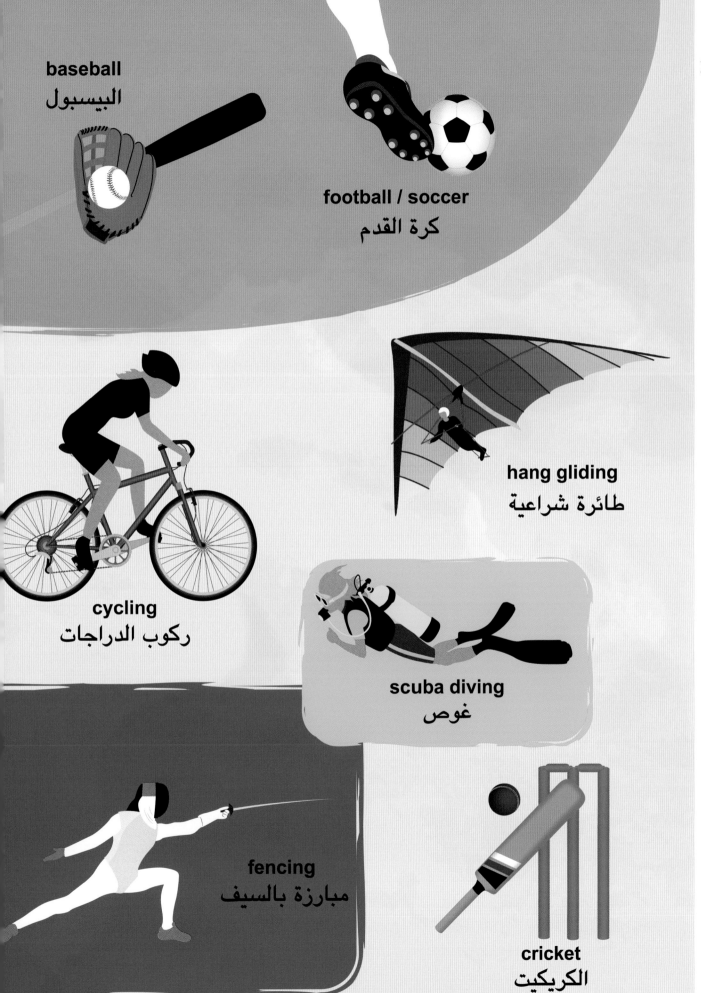

baseball
البيسبول

football / soccer
كرة القدم

hang gliding
طائرة شراعية

cycling
ركوب الدراجات

scuba diving
غوص

fencing
مبارزة بالسيف

cricket
الكريكيت

marathon
سباق المسافات الطويلة

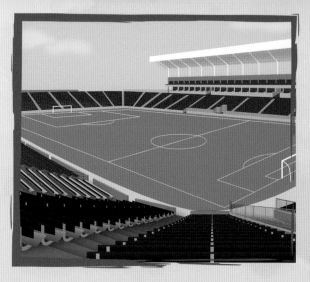

stadium
مدرج الألعاب الرياضية

sprint
جري

high jump
الوثب العالي

javelin throw
رياضة رمي المرح

hurdles
سباق الحواجز

waterpolo
كرة الماء

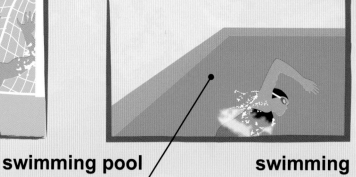

swimming pool
حوض سباحة

swimming
السباحة

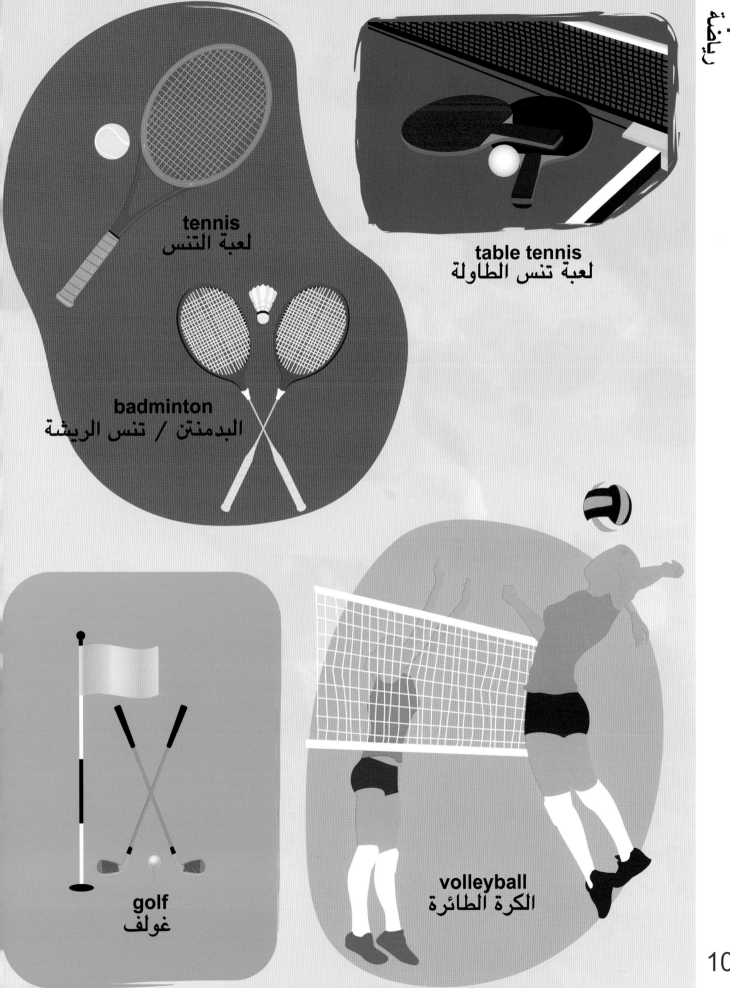

tennis
لعبة التنس

table tennis
لعبة تنس الطاولة

badminton
البدمنتن / تنس الريشة

golf
غولف

volleyball
الكرة الطائرة

mountain climbing
رياضة تسلّق الجبال

snowboarding
التزلج على الجليد

skiing
تزلّج

ice hockey
الهوكي على الجليد

rowing
تجذيف

sailing
الإبحار

rafting
رياضة التجذيف الجماعي

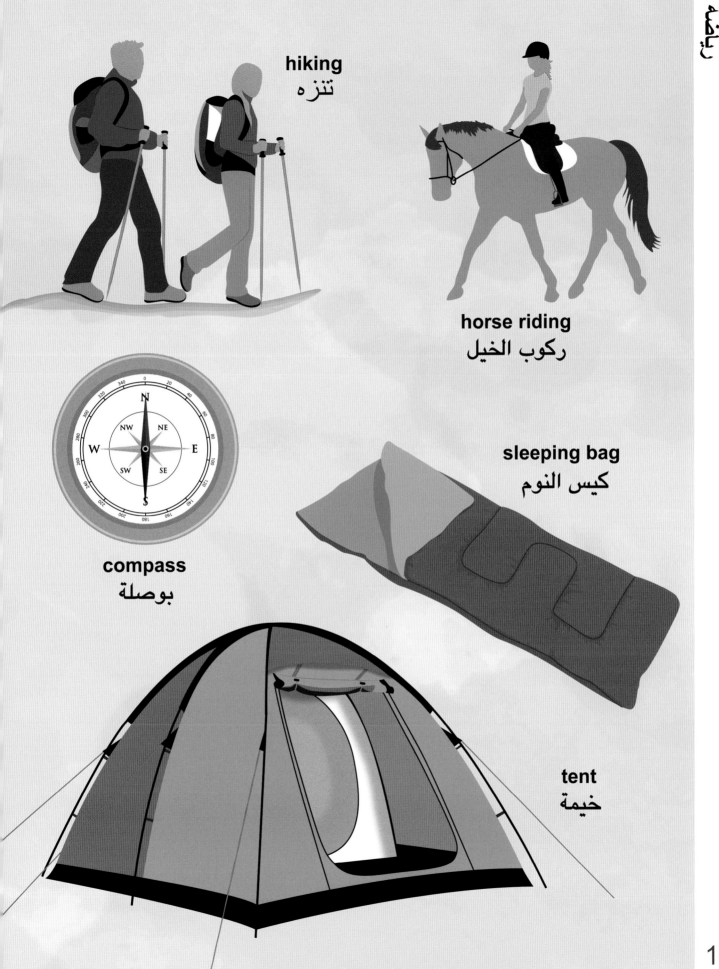

hiking
تنزه

horse riding
ركوب الخيل

compass
بوصلة

sleeping bag
كيس النوم

tent
خيمة

canvas
لوحة قماشية

painting
لوحة

palette
لوح ألوان الرسام

frame
إطار صورة

bust
تمثال نصفي

easel
حامل لقماشة
الرسام

ballet
باليه

sculpture
منحوتة

auditorium
قاعة الاستماع

orchestra
أوركسترا

stage
خشبة المسرح

concert حفلة موسيقية   **audience** جمهور

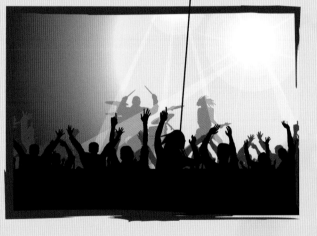

cinema سينما

CINEMA

TICKETS

museum متحف

theater مسرح

banjo
بانجو

mandolin
آلة المندولين

acoustic guitar
غيتار صوتي

harmonica
هارمونيكا

harp
قيثارة

electric guitar
غيتار كهربائي

piano
بيانو

accordion
أكورديون

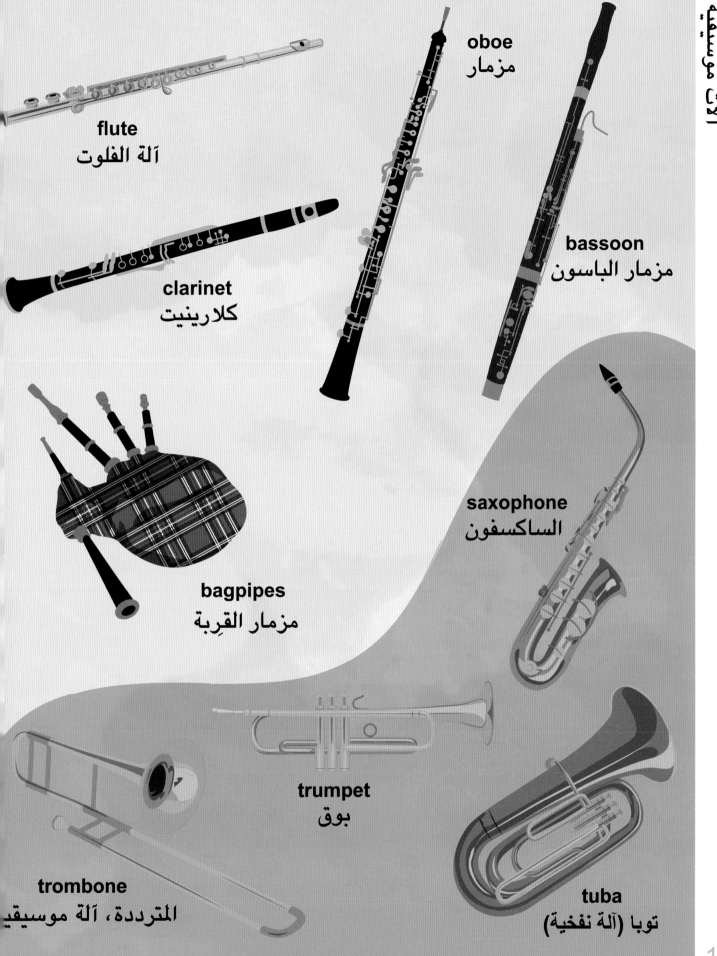

flute
آلة الفلوت

oboe
مزمار

bassoon
مزمار الباسون

clarinet
كلارينيت

bagpipes
مزمار القِربة

saxophone
الساكسفون

trumpet
بوق

trombone
المترددة، آلة موسيقية

tuba
توبا (آلة نفخية)

drum kit
مجموعة طبول

snare drum
طبل ذو صوت حاد

cymbal
الصنج

bass drum
الطبلة العظمى

drumsticks
مضارب الطبل

tambourine
دف صغير

bongo drums
طبول بونغو

music stand
حامل للنوتة الموسيقية

metronome
بندول الإيقاع

tuning fork
الشوكة الرنانة

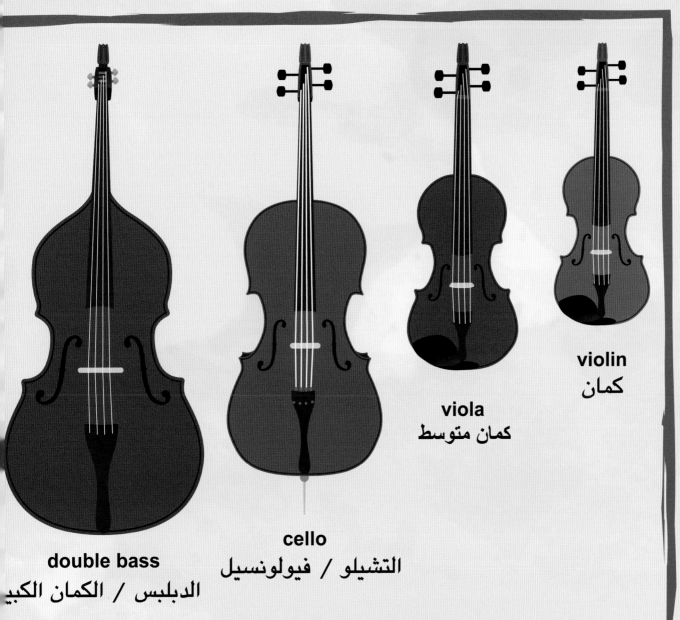

violin
كمان

viola
كمان متوسط

cello
التشيلو / فيولونسيل

double bass
الدبلبس / الكمان الكبير

one o'clock
الساعة الواحدة

hour hand
عقرب الساعات

minute hand
عقرب الدقائق

second hand
عقرب الثوان

**one fifteen /
quarter past one**
الساعة الواحدة والربع

**one thirty /
half past one**
الساعة الواحدة والنصف

**one forty-five /
quarter to two**
الساعة الثانية إلا ربع

dawn
فجر

sunrise
الشروق

evening
مساء

dusk
غسق

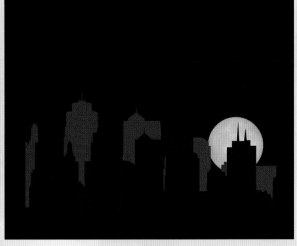

night
ليل

midnight
منتصف الليل

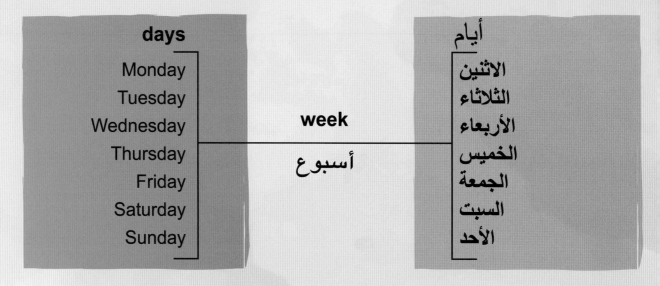

days		أيام
Monday		الاثنين
Tuesday		الثلاثاء
Wednesday	**week**	الأربعاء
Thursday	أسبوع	الخميس
Friday		الجمعة
Saturday		السبت
Sunday		الأحد

months		أشهر
January		كانون ثاني
February		شباط
March		آذار
April		نيسان
May		أيار
June	**year**	حزيران
July	سنة	تموز
August		آب
September		أيلول
October		تشرين أول
November		تشرين ثاني
December		كانون أول

2016
2026
decade
عقد

2016
2116
century
قرن

2016
3016
millennium
ألفية

seasons
فصول

spring
فصل الربيع

summer
فصل الصيف

fall
فصل الخريف

winter
فصل الشتاء

classroom
فصل دراسي

desk
مكتب

whiteboard
سبّورة

library
مكتبة

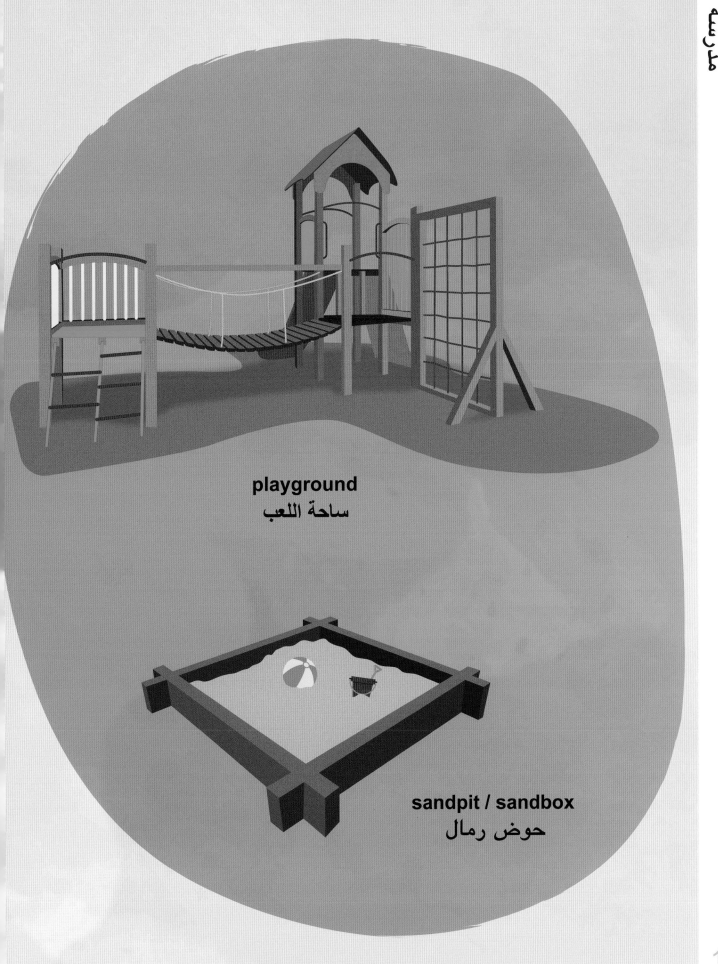

playground
ساحة اللعب

sandpit / sandbox
حوض رمال

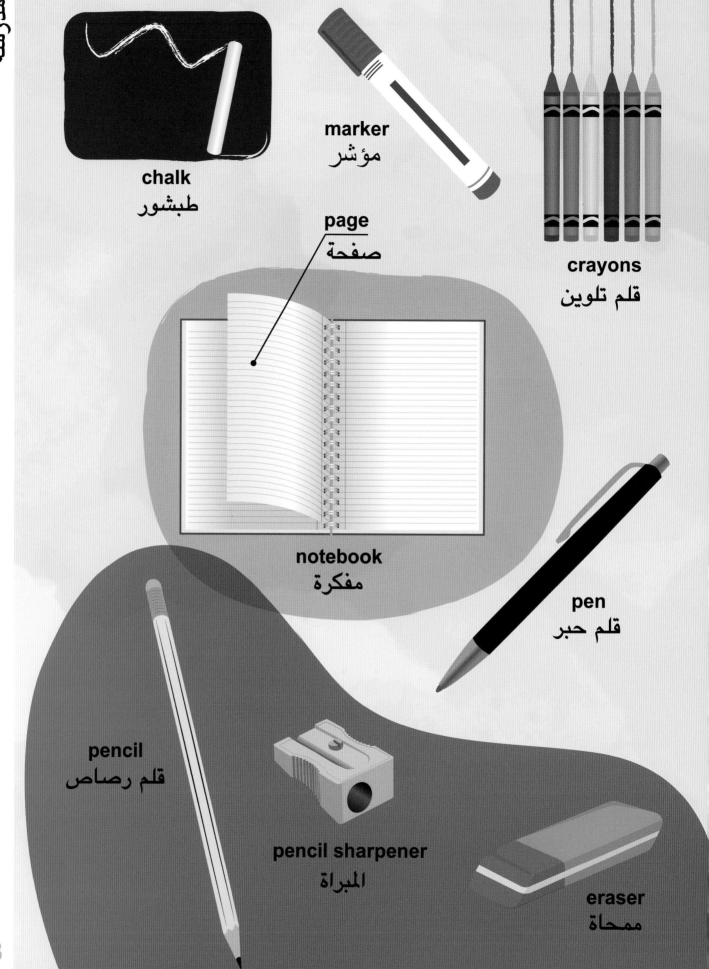

chalk
طبشور

marker
مؤشر

crayons
قلم تلوين

page
صفحة

notebook
مفكرة

pen
قلم حبر

pencil
قلم رصاص

pencil sharpener
المبراة

eraser
ممحاة

hole puncher
مكبس ثقب الورق

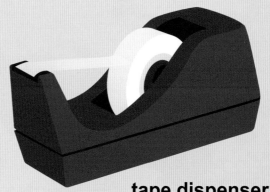

tape dispenser
موزع الشريط اللاصق

staple remover
مزيل مشبك الورق

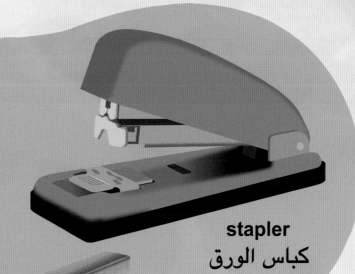

stapler
كباس الورق

staple
مشبك ورق سلكي

pushpin
دبوس تثبيت

paperclip
مشبك أوراق

scissors
مقص

119

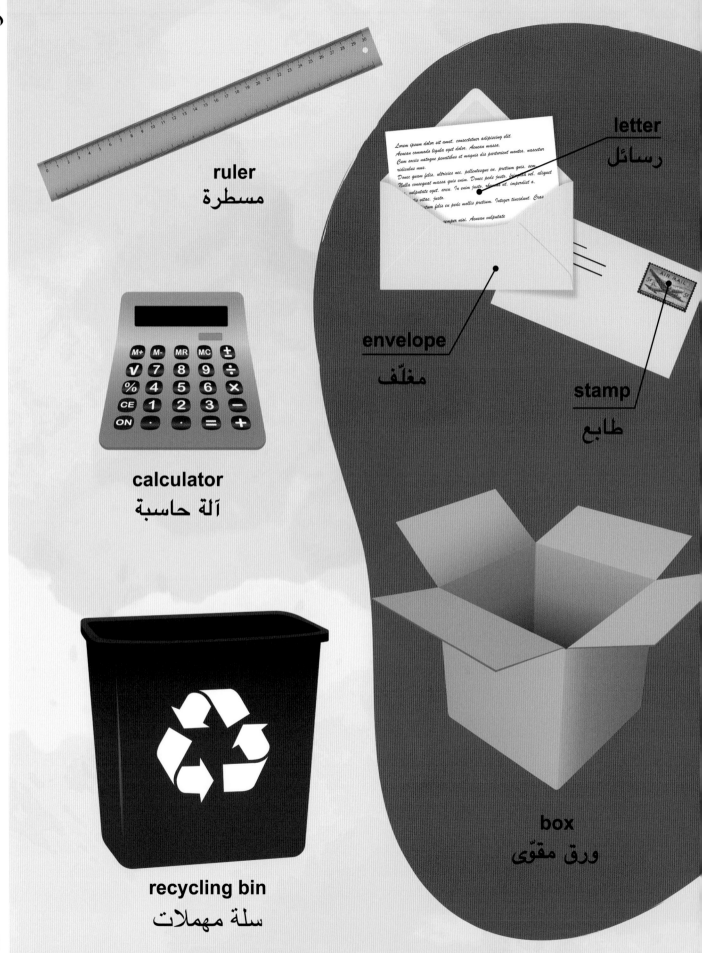

ruler
مسطرة

calculator
آلة حاسبة

recycling bin
سلة مهملات

letter
رسائل

envelope
مغلّف

stamp
طابع

box
ورق مقوّى

globe
الكرة الأرضية

telescope
منظار

microscope
مجهر

magnifying glass
عدسة مكبّرة

magnet
مغناطيس

Numbers الأرقام

0
zero
صفر

1ˢᵗ
first
أول

1
one
واحد

2
2ⁿᵈ
second
الثاني
two
إثنان

3 **3**ʳᵈ
third
الثالث
three
ثلاثة

4 **4**ᵗʰ
fourth
الرابع
four
أربعة

122

5th
fifth
الخامس

five
خمسة

6th
sixth
السادس

six
ستة

7th
seventh
السابع

seven
سبعة

8th
eighth
الثامن

eight
ثمانية

9th
ninth
التاسع

nine
تسعة

10
ten
عشرة

10th
tenth
العاشر

11
eleven
أحد عشر

11th
eleventh
الحادي عشر

12
twelve
إثنا عشر

12th
twelfth
الثاني عشر

13
thirteen
ثلاثة عشر

13th
thirteenth
الثالث عشر

14
fourteen
أربعة عشر

14th
fourteenth
الرابع عشر

15
fifteen
خمسة عشر
15th
fifteenth
الخامس عشر

16
sixteen
ستة عشر
16th
sixteenth
السادس عشر

17
seventeen
سبعة عشر
17th
seventeenth
السابع عشر

18
eighteen
ثمانية عشر
18th
eighteenth
الثامن عشر

19
nineteen
تسعة عشر
19th
nineteenth
التاسع عشر

20 twenty عشرون

20th twentieth العشرون

30 thirty ثلاثون

30th thirtieth الثلاثون

40 forty أربعون

40th fortieth الأربعون

50 fifty خمسون

50th fiftieth الخمسون

60 sixty ستون

60th sixtieth الستون

70 seventy سبعون

70th seventieth السبعون

80 eighty ثمانون

90 ninety تسعون

80th eightieth الثامن عشر

90th ninetieth التسعون

100 one hundred مئة

100th one hundredth المئة

200 two hundred مئتان

500 five hundred خمسمائة

800 eight hundred ثمانمائة

1,000 one thousand ألف

100,000 one hundred thousand مئة ألف

1,000,000 one million مليون

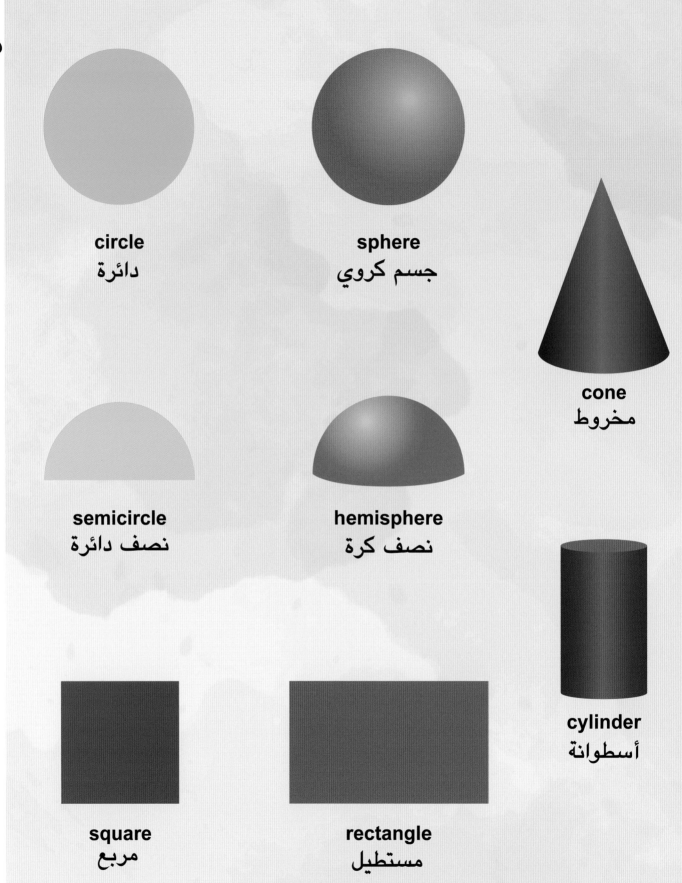

circle
دائرة

sphere
جسم كروي

cone
مخروط

semicircle
نصف دائرة

hemisphere
نصف كرة

cylinder
أسطوانة

square
مربع

rectangle
مستطيل

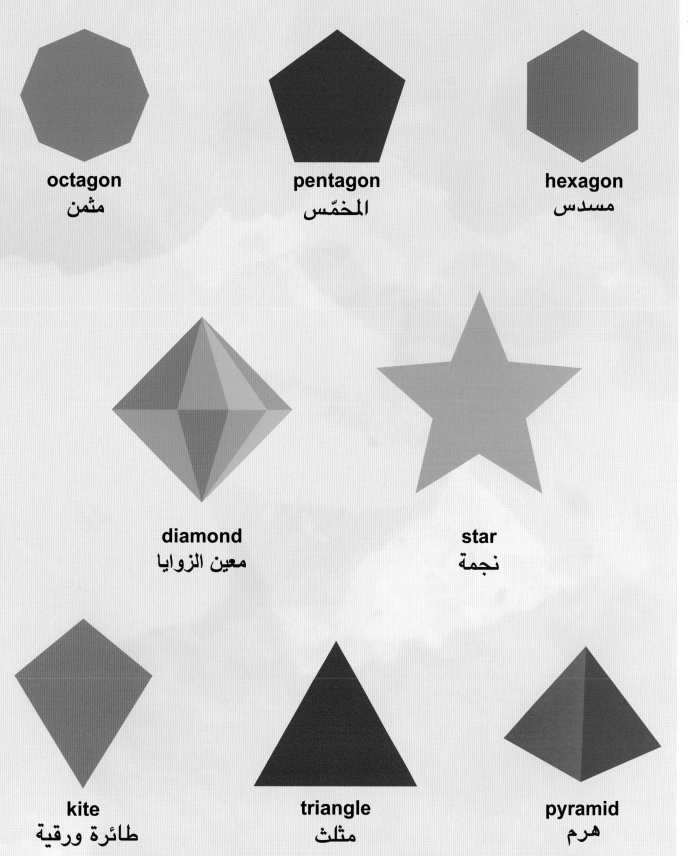

octagon
مثمن

pentagon
المخمّس

hexagon
مسدس

diamond
معين الزوايا

star
نجمة

kite
طائرة ورقية

triangle
مثلث

pyramid
هرم

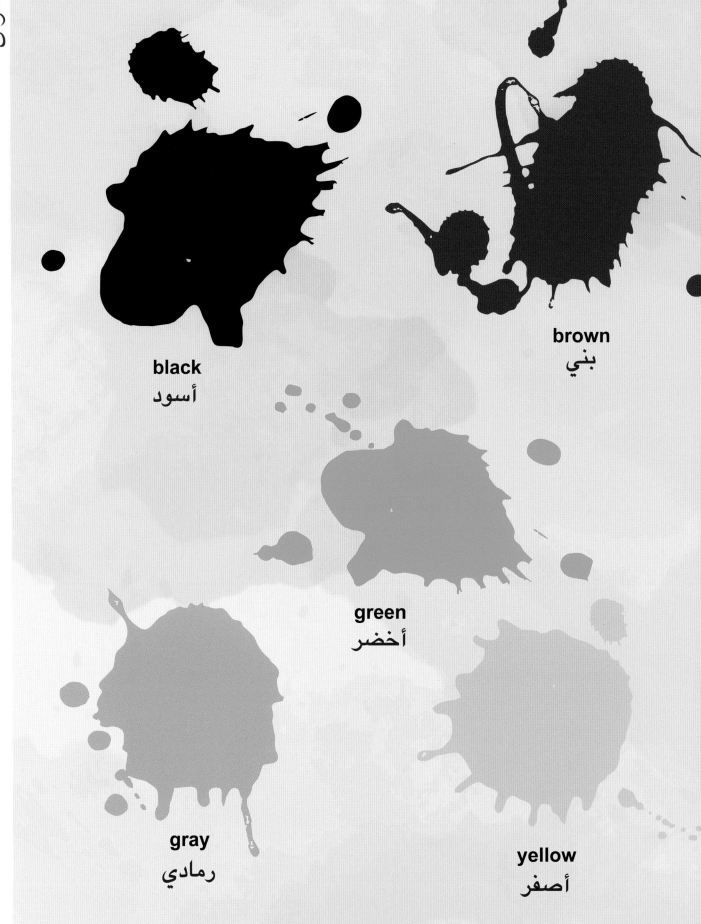

black
أسود

brown
بني

green
أخضر

gray
رمادي

yellow
أصفر

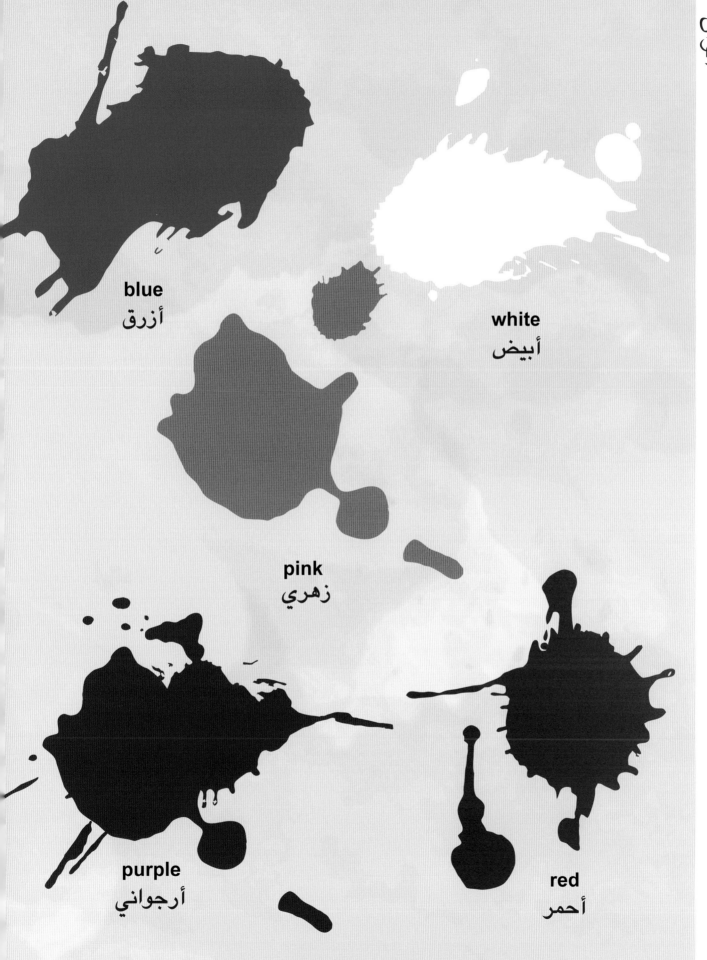

blue
أزرق

white
أبيض

pink
زهري

purple
أرجواني

red
أحمر

It's
apostrophe
الفاصلة العليا

Yes,
comma
فاصلة

like:
colon
نقطتان

self-confidence
hyphen
قاطعة

after...
ellipsis
علامة الحذف في الكتابة

won!
exclamation point
إشارة تعجب

When?
question mark
إشارة استفهام

end.
period
نقظة

"One day,"
quotation marks
علامات الاقتباس

(almost)
parentheses
قوسان بين الكلام

'good'
single quotation mark
علامات اقتباس مفردة

open;
semicolon
فارزة منقوطة

3+1

plus sign

إشارة الجمع

7-3

minus sign

إشارة الطرح

8÷2

division sign

علامة التقسيم

2×2

multiplication sign

إشارة الضرب

$\sqrt{16}$

square root sign

الجذر التربيعي

=4

equal sign

علامة المساواة

25%

percent sign

في المئة

earth & space

ampersand

حرف عطف

he/she/they

forward slash

مائل

html\n

backslash

مائل

info@milet.com

at sign

علامة @

accordion	108	begonia	82	carrot	58
acoustic guitar	108	belt	39	cat	7
adjustable wrench	48	bench	26	caterpillar	10
Africa	97	bicycle	75	cauliflower	60
air conditioner	35	birdcage	6	cave	91
airplane	76	biscuit	63	ceiling	25
airport	80	black	130	ceiling fan	34
almond	64	blackberry	56	ceiling lamp	28
ambulance	74	blanket	26	celery	61
American football	100	blender	32	cello	111
ampersand	133	blouse	38	century	114
ankle	23	blue	131	chain	50
ant	11	blueberry	56	chair	28
Antarctica	96	body	21	chalk	118
apartment building	24	bongo drums	110	chameleon	13
apostrophe	132	boots	41	chandelier	34
apple	55	bottle	30	cheek	22
apricot	56	bow tie	38	cheese	70
archery	100	bowl	29	cherry	56
arm	21	box	120	chest	21
armchair	25	bracelet	44	chestnut	64
armpit	21	brake	75	chick	7
artichoke	60	branch	87	chicken	65
Asia	97	bread	62	chili pepper	58
asparagus	61	breakfast	69	chimney	24
astronaut	99	bridge	81	chimpanzee	18
at sign	133	briefcase	45	chin	22
attic	24	broccoli	60	chips/fries	68
aubergine	60	broom	36	chisel	51
audience	107	brown	130	chocolate	69
auditorium	107	bucket	36	chocolate chip cookie	63
Australia	97	bud	82	cinema	107
avalanche	95	bull	9	circle	128
avocado	56	bulldozer	74	clarinet	109
axe	51	burger	62	classroom	116
backpack	45	burner	31	claw	6
backslash	133	bus	76	cliff	89
badminton	103	bus stop	80	clock	37
bagpipes	109	bush	87	clothes hanger	42
ballet	106	bust	106	clothespin	36
banana	56	butter	70	cloud	95
banjo	108	butterfly	11	coast	89
barn	9, 88	button	42	coat	41
barrette	46	cabbage	60	coconut	57
baseball	101	cabinet	28, 29	coffee	71
basket	37	cable	53	collar	7
basketball	100	cactus	86	colon	132
bass drum	110	cake	63	comb	46
bassoon	109	calculator	120	combination wrenches	48
bat	16	calf	9, 23	comma	132
bathrobe	40	camel	8	compass	105
bathroom	27	camellia	82	computer	52
bathtub	27	candy	69	concert	107
battery	50	candle	36	cone	128
beach	89	canned food	67	container ship	78
beak	6	canoe	79	coral	14
beans	66	canvas	106	corn	58
bear	17	cap	39	corncob	58
bed	26	car	72	cotton	82
bedroom	26	car battery	50	countryside	88
bee	10	cardigan	40	courgette	60
beehive	10	carnation	82	cow	9
beetle	10	carpet	26	crab	15

crackers	63	easel	106	flood	94
crayfish	15	egg	6, 66	floor	25
crayons	118	egg white	66	floor lamp	34
crest	7	eight	123	flour	62
cricket	10	eight hundred	127	flowerpot	37
cricket	101	eighteen	125	flute	109
crocodile	13	eighteenth	125	fly	11
crosswalk	80	eighth	123	folding chair	25
crow	5	eightieth	127	food processor	32
cruise ship	78	eighty	127	foot	21
cub	19	elbow	23	footprint	23
cucumber	58	electric drill	50	forehead	22
curtain	25	electric guitar	108	forest	90
cushion	25	electric razor	47	fork	30
cuticle nipper	46	electrical outlet	35	forklift	74
cutting board	30	elephant	17	fortieth	126
cycling	101	eleven	124	forty	126
cylinder	128	eleventh	124	forward slash	133
cymbal	110	ellipsis	132	fossil	92
daffodil	84	ember	94	four	122
daisy	82	emerald	44	fourteen	124
dam	90	emery board	46	fourteenth	124
dawn	113	engine	72	fourth	122
decade	114	envelope	120	fox	17
deer	18	equal sign	133	frame	106
desert	91	eraser	118	freight truck	73
desk	116	Europe	96	frog	12
desk lamp	34	evening	113	frost	95
dessert	69	exclamation point	132	fruit juice	71
diamond	44, 129	eye	22	frying pan	29
digger	74	eye glasses	43	fuchsia	82
dill	61	eyebrow	22	fuel flap	72
dining table	28	eyelashes	22	galaxy	99
disaster	94	eyelid	22	garage	81
dishwasher	33	face	22	garden	87
division sign	133	falcon	4	gardenia	83
dog	7	fall	115	garlic	58
dolphin	15	farm	88	gas pump	81
donkey	8	faucet	27	gas station	81
door	24	faucet	31	geranium	83
door buzzer	35	fawn	18	giraffe	19
door handle	35	feather	6	glass	30
doorbell	35	fencing	101	globe	121
doormat	37	fender	72	glove	41
double bass	111	field	88	goat	9
dragonfly	11	fifteen	125	golf	103
drawer	29	fifteenth	125	goose	8
dress	38	fifth	123	gorilla	18
drill bit	49	fiftieth	126	grape	55
drum kit	110	fifty	126	grapefruit	57
drumsticks	110	finger	21	grape tree	86
duck	8	fingernail	22	grasshopper	11
dump truck	73	fingerprint	22	gray	130
dusk	113	fire	94	green	130
dust cloth	26	fire truck	74	green bean	59
duster	33	fireplace	25	grill	72
eagle	4	first	122	ground beef	65
ear	22	fish	15, 65	ground floor	24
earphones	53	five	123	gull	4
earrings	44	five hundred	127	hair	22
Earth	98	flame	94	hair dryer	47
earthquake	94	flamingo	4	hairbrush	46
earthworm	12	flip-flops	40	half past one	112

hammer	48
hand	21, 22
hand bag	45
hand gliding	101
handlebars	75
handsaw	51
harmonica	108
harp	108
harvest	88
hat	38
hay	88
hazelnut	64
head	21
headlight	72
hedgehog	20
heel	23
helicopter	76
hemisphere	128
hen	7
heron	4
hexagon	129
high jump	102
highway	80
hiking	105
hill	93
hip	23
hippopotamus	18
hole puncher	119
honey	67
hood	72
horn	18
horse	8
horse riding	105
hose	51
hour hand	112
house	24
hurdles	102
hurricane	94
hyacinth	83
hyphen	132
ice cream	69
ice cube	71
ice hockey	104
icicle	95
iguana	12
index finger	22
iris	83
iron	33
ironing board	36
island	89
jar	30
jasmine	83
javelin	102
jeans	39
jellyfish	15
jerrycan	37
jet ski	79
jewellery	44
judo	100
juicer	30
jungle	91
Jupiter	98
kangaroo	16
key	35
keyboard	52
kitchen	29
kite	129
kitten	7
kiwi	57
knee	21
knife	30
koala	16
ladder	50
ladybird	11
lake	89
lamb	9
lavender	83
leaf	87
leek	61
leg	21
lemon	55
lemonade	71
lentils	66
leopard	19
letter	120
lettuce	60
library	116
lighter	31
lightning	95
lilac	84
lion	19
lip	22
little finger	22
living room	25
lizard	13
llama	16
lobster	14
log	87
long-nose pliers	49
lovebird	5
magnet	121
magnifying glass	121
magnolia	84
mallet	49
mandarin	57
mandolin	108
mane	19
mango	57
manicure set	46
marathon	102
marker	118
Mars	98
melon	57
Mercury	98
metronome	111
microphone	53
microscope	121
microwave oven	32
middle finger	22
midnight	113
milk	70
millennium	114
minivan	73
mint	61
minus sign	133
minute hand	112
mirror	27
mixer	32
mobile phone	53
mole	20
mole wrench	48
monitor	52
month	114
Moon	98
mop	36
mosquito	11
moss	84
moth	11
motorcycle	75
mountain	92
mountain climbing	104
mouse	20, 52
mouth	22
mud	95
multiplication sign	133
museum	107
mushroom	58
music stand	111
nail	49
nail clippers	46
nail file	46
navel	23
neck	22
necklace	44
Neptune	98
nest	6
nettle	84
newspaper	53
newt	12
night	113
night stand	26
nine	123
nineteen	125
nineteenth	125
ninetieth	127
ninety	127
ninth	123
North America	96
nose	22
notebook	118
nut	49
oats	86
oboe	109
ocean	89
octagon	129
octopus	15
oil	67
okra	59
olive	67
olive oil	67
one	122
one hundred	127
one hundrendth	127
one hundred thousand	127
one million	127
one o'clock	112
one thousand	127
onion	59
open ended wrench	48

orange	55	plus sign	133	rowing	104
orange juice	71	pocket	39	rubbish bag/garbage bag	37
orchestra	107	polar bear	17	ruby	44
orchid	85	police car	74	rug	25
ostrich	5	pomegranate	57	ruler	120
otter	20	popcorn	69	rye	86
oven	29	poppy	84	saddle	75
owl	6	port	81	safety helmet	50
padlock	50	pot	29	safety pin	42
page	118	potato	59	sail	79
painting	106	printer	52	sailboat	79
palm	21	puddle	95	sailing	104
palm tree	86	pumpkin	59	salad	68
pancakes	63	pumps	38	salamander	12
panda	17	puppy	7	salt	68
paper-clip	119	purple	131	sand	89
parentheses	132	purse	43	sandals	39
parrot	6	pushpin	119	sandpit/sandbox	117
parsley	61	pyramid	129	sandwich	62
passport	43	quarter past one	112	satellite dish	99
pasta	66	quarter to two	112	Saturn	98
path	90	question mark	132	sausage	65
peach	56	quince	57	saxophone	109
peacock	5	quotation marks	132	scale	31
peanut	64	rabbit	20	scanner	52
pear	55	raccoon	16	scarf	41
peas	59	race car	74	scissors	46
pebbles	93	radiator	35	scissors	119
pedal	75	radio	53	scooter	75
pelican	4	radish	61	scorpion	10
pen	118	rafting	104	screw	49
pencil	118	railroad station	81	screwdriver	49
pencil sharpener	118	railroad track	81	scuba diving	101
penguin	15	rain	95	sculpture	106
pentagon	129	rake	51	seahorse	14
pepper	58	range hood	29	seal	15
pepper	68	raspberry	56	seaweed	14
percent	133	rat	20	second	122
perfume	47	razor	47	second hand	112
period	132	recriotional vehicle	73	semicircle	128
pet	7	rectangle	128	semicolon	132
pet bed	7	recycling bin	120	seven	123
petal	83	red	131	seventeen	125
piano	108	reel	42	seventeenth	125
pick	51	refrigerator	29	seventieth	126
pickup truck	73	restaurant	54	seventh	123
pie	63	rhinoceros	18	seventy	126
pier	81	ribbon	42	sewing needle	42
pig	9	rice	66	shaker	31
pigeon	5	ring	44	shaving brush	47
pillow	26	ring finger	22	sheep	9
pine cone	86	river	92	sheet	26
pineapple	55	road	80	shelf	27
pink	131	robin	5	shin	23
pins	42	rock	93	shirt	39
pistachio	64	rocking chair	25	shoelaces	39
pitcher	31	rock layer	93	shoes	38
pizza	62	roof	24	shorts	39
place setting	28	rooster	7	shoulder	23
plate	30	root	87	shovel	51
playground	117	rope	51	shower	27
plug	50	rose	85	sidewalk	80
plum	55	row boat	79	single quotation marks	132

sink	27
sink	31
six	123
sixteen	125
sixteenth	125
sixth	123
sixtieth	126
sixty	126
skeleton	23
skiing	104
skirt	38
skull	23
skunk	16
sled	75
sleeping bag	105
slice of bread	62
slip joint pliers	48
slippers	40
slope	93
slow cooker	29
snacks	68
snail	10
snake	12
snapdragon	84
snare drum	110
sneakers	39
snow	95
snowboarding	104
snowdrop	85
soap	27
soccer	101
socks	41
sofa	25
soil	92
solar system	98
soup	68
South America	96
soy milk	70
space	98
space shuttle	99
space station	99
sparrow	6
spatula	31
speaker	52
sphere	128
spider	11
spinach	61
spirit level	48
spoke	75
sponge	27
spoon	30
spotlight	34
spring	115
spring onion	61
sprint	102
square	128
square root of	133
squirrel	20
stadium	102
stage	107
stamp	120
staple remover	119
stapler	119
staples	119
star	129
starfish	14
steak	65
steering wheel	72
steps	24
stomach	21
stone	93
stool	28
storage box	36
stork	5
strawberry	56
street	80
stroller	75
sugar	69
suit	38
suitcase	45
summer	115
Sun	92, 98
sunflower	85
sunglasses	43
sunrise	113
supermarket	54
swallow	5
swan	4
sweater	40
swimming	102
swimming pool	102
swimming trunks	40
swimsuit	40
T-shirt	39
table lamp	34
tablet	53
tableware	28
tadpole	12
tail	6, 20
tambourine	110
tape dispenser	119
tape measure	49
tea	71
teapot	31
teaspoon	31
telephone	53
telescope	121
ten	124
tennis	103
tent	105
tenth	124
theater	107
thigh	21
third	122
thirteen	124
thirteenth	124
thirtieth	126
thirty	126
thread	42
three	122
thumb	22
tie	38
tiger	19
tire	72
toad	13
toast	62
toaster	32
toaster oven	32
toe	21
toilet	27
toilet paper	27
tomato	59
toolbox	50
toothbrush	47
toothpaste	47
torch	50
tornado	94
tortoise	13
tow truck	73
towel	27
tracksuit	41
tractor	74
traffic	80
traffic light	80
train	77
tram	77
tree	87
triangle	129
trombone	109
trousers	41
truck	73
trumpet	109
trunk	17, 72, 87
tuba	109
tulip	85
tuning fork	111
turkey	8
turnip	61
turtle	14
tusk	17
tweezers	46
twelfth	124
twelve	124
twentieth	126
twenty	126
two	122
two hundred	127
umbrella	45
underground	77
Uranus	98
vacuum cleaner	33
valley	93
van	73
vase	37
Venus	98
video camera	53
viola	111
violin	111
volcano	93
volleyball	103
vulture	6
waist	21
wall	24
wallet	43
walnut	64
walrus	14
wardrobe	26
washing machine	33
wasp	10

watch	44
water	71
water lily	85
water polo	102
waterfall	90
watermelon	55
wave	89
web	11
week	114
weightlifting	100
wetland	90
wheat	86
wheel	75
wheelbarrow	51
white	131
whiteboard	116
window	24
windscreen	72
wipers	72
wing	6
wing	76
winter	115
wolf	17
wood	87
woodpecker	6
wrestling	100
wrist	22
yacht	78
year	114
yellow	130
yogurt	70
yolk	66
zebra	18
zero	122
zipper	42